ㅛ	요 / *yo*	
ㅜ	우 / *u*	문학 *munhak* / literature
ㅠ	유 / *yu*	규칙 *gyuchik* / rule 유럽 *yureop* / Europe
ㅡ	으 / *eu*	금요일 *geumyoil* / Friday 음식 *eumsik* / food
ㅣ	이 / *i*	필통 *piltong* / pencil case 입 *ip* / mouth
ㅐ	애 / *ae*	앨범 *aelbeom* / album 새 *sae* / bird
ㅒ	얘 / *yae*	얘들아 *yaedeura* / guys 걔 *gyae* / that person
ㅔ	에 / *e*	게임 *geim* / game 케이크 *keikeu* / cake
ㅖ	예 / *ye*	예산 *yesan* / budget 계단 *gyedan* / stairs
ㅘ	와 / *wa*	화요일 *hwayoil* / Tuesday 와플 *wapeul* / waffle
ㅙ	왜 / *wae*	돼지 *dwaeji* / pig 횃불 *hwaetbul* / torch
ㅚ	외 / *oe*	회사 *hoesa* / company 외국 *oeguk* / foreign country
ㅝ	워 / *wo*	원숭이 *wonsungi* / monkey 월 *wol* / month

ㅞ	웨 / we	웨딩 *weding* / wedding 웹사이트 *wepsaiteu* / website
ㅟ	위 / wi	귀 *gwi* / ear 퀴즈 *kwijeu* / quiz
ㅢ	의 / ui	의사 *uisa* / doctor 희망 *huimang* / hope

• Making Syllables

	ㅏ a	ㅓ eo	ㅗ o	ㅜ u	ㅡ eu	ㅣ i
ㄱ g/k	가 *ga*	거 *geo*	고 *go*	구 *gu*	그 *geu*	기 *gi*
ㄴ n	나 *na*	너 *neo*	노 *no*	누 *nu*	느 *neu*	니 *ni*
ㄷ d/t	다 *da*	더 *deo*	도 *do*	두 *du*	드 *deu*	디 *di*
ㄹ r/l	라 *ra*	러 *reo*	로 *ro*	루 *ru*	르 *reu*	리 *ri*
ㅁ m	마 *ma*	머 *meo*	모 *mo*	무 *mu*	므 *meu*	미 *mi*
ㅂ b/p	바 *ba*	버 *beo*	보 *bo*	부 *bu*	브 *beu*	비 *bi*
ㅅ s	사 *sa*	서 *seo*	소 *so*	수 *su*	스 *seu*	시 *si*
ㅇ ∅/ng	아 *a*	어 *eo*	오 *o*	우 *u*	으 *eu*	이 *i*
ㅈ j	자 *ja*	저 *jeo*	조 *jo*	주 *ju*	즈 *jeu*	지 *ji*
ㅊ ch	차 *cha*	처 *cheo*	초 *cho*	추 *chu*	츠 *cheu*	치 *chi*
ㅋ k	카 *ka*	커 *keo*	코 *ko*	쿠 *ku*	크 *keu*	키 *ki*
ㅌ t	타 *ta*	터 *teo*	토 *to*	투 *tu*	트 *teu*	티 *ti*
ㅍ p	파 *pa*	퍼 *peo*	포 *po*	푸 *pu*	프 *peu*	피 *pi*
ㅎ h	하 *ha*	허 *heo*	호 *ho*	후 *hu*	흐 *heu*	히 *hi*

Chapter 1

Everyday Essentials

When you arrive in Korea, there are some phrases and words that you will encounter often. In this chapter, we have listed a quick overview of everyday essentials to get you going. We also introduce forms of address towards Korean people and the Korean numeral system, so it will be very helpful to read this part thoroughly.

Some useful websites for your stay in Korea are Daum and Naver. Both Daum and Naver have search toolbars through which you can find anything from popular restaurants to shopping malls. Naver additionally has a very detailed map of Korea and an English-Korean dictionary, which are also available as smartphone apps. However, there is no need to worry if you are just starting out with learning Korean. Koreans will already be delighted if you are able to say 안녕하세요 (Hello)!

Useful Words

First, there are some crucial words that you should know when first entering Korea:

passport | 여권 *yeogwon*
visa | 비자 *bija*
alien registration card | 외국인 등록증 *oegugin deungnokjeung*
baggage | 짐 *jim*
phone number | 전화번호 *jeonhwabeonho*
person | 사람 *saram*
money | 돈 *don*
won | 원 *won*
man | 남자 *namja*
woman | 여자 *yeoja*

TIP

In Korea, people don't use WhatsApp. Instead, they use a Korean messaging application called KakaoTalk. If you go to Korea, make sure to download it!

Greetings

hello | 안녕하세요 *annyeonghaseyo*

goodbye (when someone is staying) | 안녕히 계세요 *annyeonghi gyeseyo*

goodbye (when someone is leaving) | 안녕히 가세요 *annyeonghi gaseyo*

long time no see | 오랜만이에요 *oraenmanieyo*

thank you (formal) | 감사합니다 *gamsahamnida*

thank you (casual) | 고맙습니다 *gomapseumnida*

I'm sorry (formal) | 죄송합니다 *joesonghamnida*

I'm sorry (casual) | 미안합니다 *mianhamnida*

excuse me (when asking for attention) | 저기요 *jeogiyo*

it's okay | 괜찮아요 *gwaenchanayo*

Useful Sentences

INTRODUCING YOURSELF

What's your name?	이름이 뭐예요? *Ireumi mwoyeyo?*
My name is Chelsey.	제 이름은 첼시예요. *Je ireumeun chelsiyeyo.*
I am Chelsey.	저는 첼시예요. *Jeoneun chelsiyeyo.*
Nice to meet you.	만나서 반갑습니다. *Mannaseo bangapseupnida.*
How old are you? (formal colloquial)	나이가 어떻게 되세요? *Naiga eotteoke doeseyo?*

How old are you? (casual)	몇 살이에요? *Myeot sarieyo?*
I am twenty-two years old.	22살이에요. *Seumul du sarieyo.*
I was born in Vancouver.	저는 밴쿠버에서 태어났어요. *Jeoneun baenkubeoeseo taeeonasseoyo.*
Let me introduce myself.	제 소개를 하겠습니다. *Je sogaereul hagetseumnida.*

LANGUAGE DIFFICULTIES

I can't speak Korean.	저는 한국어를 못해요. *Jeoneun hangugeoreul motaeyo.*
Please speak slower.	더 천천히 말씀해 주세요. *Deo cheoncheonhi malsseumhae juseyo.*
Please speak louder.	더 크게 말씀해 주세요. *Deo keuge malsseumhae juseyo.*
Please say that again.	다시 한 번 말씀해 주세요. *Dasi han beon malsseumhae juseyo.*
Can you speak English?	영어 할 줄 아세요? *Yeongeo hal jul aseyo?*
I (can't) understand you.	(못) 알아 들었어요. *(Mot) Ara deureosseoyo.*

What does this mean?	이건 무슨 뜻이에요? *Igeon museun tteusieyo?*
What is this in Korean?	이건 한국어로 뭐예요? *Igeon hangugeoro mwoyeyo?*

MISCELLANEOUS

I know.	알아요. *Arayo.*
I don't know.	몰라요. *Mollayo.*
Yes.	예. *Ye.* / 네. *Ne.*
No.	아니오. *Anio.*
Where is the toilet?	화장실은 어디 있어요? *Hwajangsireun eodi isseoyo?*
Please give me an Americano.	아메리카노 한 잔 주세요. *Amerikano han jan juseyo.*
What are you doing?	지금 뭐해요? *Jigeum mwohaeyo?*
What is this?	이건 뭐예요? *Igeon mwoyeyo?*
Congratulations!	축하해요! *Chukahaeyo!*

Happy birthday!	생일 축하해요! *Saengil chukahaeyo!*

Countries

country | 국가 *gukga*, 나라 *nara*
Korea | 한국 *hanguk*
China | 중국 *jungguk*
Japan | 일본 *ilbon*
U.S.A | 미국 *miguk*
Australia | 호주 *hoju*
France | 프랑스 *peurangseu*
Germany | 독일 *dogil*
England | 영국 *yeongguk*
Russia | 러시아 *reosia*

Useful Expressions

I am from America.	저는 미국에서 왔어요. *Jeoneun migugeseo wasseoyo.*
I am English.	저는 영국인이에요. *Jeoneun yeongguginieyo.*
I am going to Korea.	저는 한국에 갈 거예요. *Jeoneun hanguge gal geoyeyo.*

Forms of Address

Mr. / Mrs. / Ms. | －씨 *ssi*

older male (for women) | 오빠 *oppa*

older woman (for women) | 언니 *eonni*

older male (for men) | 형 *hyeong*

older woman (for men) | 누나 *nuna*

middle-aged woman | 아줌마 *ajumma*, 아주머니 *ajumeoni*

middle-aged man | 아저씨 *ajeossi*

parents | 부모님 *bumonim*

mother | 어머니 *eomeoni*, 엄마 *eomma*

father | 아버지 *abeoji*, 아빠 *appa*

younger man (younger brother) | 남동생 *namdongsaeng*

younger woman (younger sister) | 여동생 *yeodongsaeng*

aunt | 이모 *imo*

uncle | 삼촌 *samchon*

Forms of address

In Korea, it is impolite to address people by just their first name; you have to address them with a word of status attached to it. Instead of saying "you," you have to say someone's name followed by a suffix of status. The word you have to use behind someone's name varies depending on how close you are to that person and what their status is compared to your status.

If you don't know someone that well, you can add a "－씨" *ssi* to their name. For example, if your name is (Lee) Jihyun, you call someone "(이)지현 씨" *(lee) jihyeon ssi*. This is a polite way to refer to someone and is the equivalent of Mr. or Mrs./Ms.

If you are talking to someone that is higher in status than you, such as a professor or a colleague in a higher position, you have to call them by their last name and add their position. So when you refer to a professor with the last name Kim, this becomes "김 교수님" *kim gyosunim*.

When you are close to a person, there are several ways to address them depending on their gender and age. In Korea, a lot of family terms are used to refer to people you know. If you are a girl, you refer to an older guy as "오빠" *oppa* and an older girl as "언니" *eonni*. If you are a guy, you refer to an older guy as "형" *hyeong* and to an older girl as "누나" *nuna*. These older guys and girls will in return call you their "동생" *dongsaeng* (younger sibling) or add the suffix "-아/야" *(a/ya)* to your name. When there is a vowel at the end of someone's name, you should add a "-야" and when there is a consonant, you should add "-아." For example, "동현아" *donghyeona* or "은지야" *eunjiya*.

Lastly, there is the category of middle-aged men and women. We refer to these people as "아줌마/아주머니" *ajumma/ajumeoni* for women and "아저씨" *ajeossi* for men. But if you want to attract the attention of the lady working in a restaurant, it is better to call her "이모" *imo* if you want to stay in her good graces.

Numbers

In Korea, there are two kinds of numeral systems: native Korean numerals and Sino-Korean numerals.

Number	Native Korean numerals	Sino-Korean numerals
1	하나 *hana*	일 *il*
2	둘 *dul*	이 *i*
3	셋 *set*	삼 *sam*
4	넷 *net*	사 *sa*
5	다섯 *daseot*	오 *o*
6	여섯 *yeoseot*	육 *yuk*
7	일곱 *ilgop*	칠 *chil*
8	여덟 *yeodeol*	팔 *pal*
9	아홉 *ahop*	구 *gu*
10	열 *yeol*	십 *sip*
11	열하나 *yeolhana*	십일 *sibil*
20	스물 *seumul*	이십 *isip*
100		백 *baek*
1,000		천 *cheon*
10,000		만 *man*
100,000		십만 *sipman*
1,000,000		백만 *baekman*
100,000,000		억 *eok*

COUNTING

Korean has specific words for counting people, animals, books, and many other things. When you count things in Korean, you often name the thing you are counting first, and then the number followed by a counter word.

Examples

eight dogs	개 8(여덟) 마리 *gae yeodeol mari*
four people	사람 4(네) 명 *saram ne myeong*

In the table below, you can find the most important counter words and the numeral system you have to use with those counter words. When you learn a new counter word, it is best to immediately learn the accompanying numeral system.

Counter words used with native Korean numerals (하나, 둘, 셋, 넷 . . .)	
people	1명 *han myeong*
animals	1마리 *han mari*
items	1개 *han gae*
volumes	1권 *han gwon*
lessons (for counting)	1과 *han gwa*
hours (for duration)	1시간 *han sigan*
months	1달 *han dal*

age	1살 *han sal*
items of clothing	1벌 *han beol*
sheets of paper	1장 *han jang*
cups	1잔 *han jan*
bottles	1병 *han byeong*
plates (dishes)	1그릇 *han geureut*

Counter words used with Sino-Korean numerals (일, 이, 삼, 사 . . .)

floors, layers	1층 *ilcheung*
lesson number	1과 *ilgwa*
won	1원 *irwon*
portions (of food)	1인분 *irinbun*
school year, grade	1학년 *ilhangnyeon*
year	1년 *ilnyeon*
month (for date)	1월 *irwol*
day (for date)	1일 *ilil*

Also, be aware that there are some words where both numeral systems can be used, but have different meanings. For example, when you are talking about the chapters of a textbook you would say "사 과" *sa gwa* (Sino-Korean) to refer to the fourth chapter, and "네 과" *ne gwa* (native Korean) to refer to four chapters.

Exceptions

When put in front of a counter word, the first four numbers in the native Korean numeral system (하나, 둘, 셋, 넷) and the number twenty (스물) change form. See the table below.

하나	한 *han*
둘	두 *du*
셋	세 *se*
넷	네 *ne*
스물	스무 *seumu*

Examples

two rabbits	토끼 2(두) 마리 *tokki du mari*
twenty people	사람 20(스무) 명 *saram seumu myeong*

Time and Dates

TIME

year | 년 *nyeon*

month | 월 *weol*

week | 주 *ju*

day | 일 *il*

hour | 시간 *sigan*

p.m. | 오후 *ohu*

a.m. | 오전 *ojeon*

minute | 분 *bun*

second | 초 *cho*

_ o'clock | _ 시 *si*

🗨 Useful Expressions

What time is it now?	지금 몇 시예요? *Jigeum myeot siyeyo?*
What time shall we meet?	몇 시에 만날까요? *Myeot sie mannalkkayo?*

💡 TIP

When referring to time, Koreans use a combination of Sino-Korean numerals and native Korean numerals. Everything pertaining to hours, such as "시간" *sigan* and "시" *si*, is used with native Korean numerals. If you want to say it is 4 o'clock, you have to say "네 시예요" *Ne sieyo*. Therefore, if you want to say that it is 3:40 p.m., you have to use both types of numerals to say "세 시 사십 분이에요" *Se si sasip bunieyo*. If you want to say it is half past five, you could say " 다섯 시 반" *daseot si ban* or "다섯 시 삼십 분" *daseot si samsip bun*, as "반" is the Korean word for "half."

DATES

Days of the week

Sunday | 일요일 *iryoil*

Monday | 월요일 *woryoil*

Tuesday | 화요일 *hwayoil*

Wednesday | 수요일 *suyoil*

Thursday | 목요일 *mogyoil*

Friday | 금요일 *geumyoil*

Saturday | 토요일 *toyoil*

When counting in Korean, you start with the biggest unit and end with the smallest. So when naming a date, you first name the year, then the month, and then the day, hour, etc.

Months

January | 1월 *irwol*

February | 2월 *iwol*

March | 3월 *samwol*

April | 4월 *sawol*

May | 5월 *owol*

June | 6월 *yuwol*

July | 7월 *chirwol*

August | 8월 *parwol*

September | 9월 *guwol*

October | 10월 *siwol*

November | 11월 *sibirwol*

December | 12월 *sibiwol*

> **TIP**
>
> For June and October, the pronunciation is a little different. For June, instead of saying "육월" *yugwol*, you say "유월" *yuwol*. For October, instead of saying "십월" *sibwol*, you say "시월" *siwol*. "년" *nyeon*, "월" *wol*, "일" *il*, "분" *bun*, and "초" *cho* are all used with Sino-Korean numerals. If you want to name a date, such as August 20, 2017, it will be "이천십칠년 팔월 이십일" *icheonsipchillyeon parwol isibil*.

Miscellaneous

this year | 올해 *olhae*

last year | 작년 *jangnyeon*

next year | 내년 *naenyeon*

today | 오늘 *oneul*

yesterday | 어제 *eoje*

tomorrow | 내일 *naeil*

the day after tomorrow | 모레 *more*

a few days | 며칠 *myeochil*

now | 지금 *jigeum*

lately | 요즘 *yojeum*

last | 지난 *jinan*

this time | 이번 *ibeon*

next time | 다음번 *daeumbeon*

first │ 첫 번째 *cheot beonjjae*

during │ 동안 *dongan*

morning │ 아침 *achim*

afternoon │ 오후 *ohu*

daytime │ 낮 *nat*

evening │ 저녁 *jeonyeok*

night │ 밤 *bam*

weekend │ 주말 *jumal*

all day long │ 하루 종일 *haru jongil*

every day │ 매일 *maeil*

every week │ 매주 *maeju*

early │ 일찍 *iljjik*

often │ 종종 *jongjong*

always │ 항상 *hangsang*

a long time │ 오랫동안 *oraetdongan*

🗨 Useful Expressions

I woke up at 9 a.m. today.	오늘 오전 9시에 일어났어요. *Oneul ojeon ahop sie ireonasseoyo.*
I went to Korea last month.	지난 달에 한국에 갔어요. *Jinan dare hanguge gasseoyo.*
I have lived in America for five years.	저는 5년 동안 미국에서 살았어요. *Jeoneun onyeon dongan migugeseo sarasseoyo.*

I have an appointment from 3 p.m. to 5 p.m. today.

오늘 오후 세 시부터 다섯 시까지 약속이 있어요.
Oneul ohu se sibuteo daseot sikkaji yaksogi isseoyo.

Seasons and Weather

season │ 계절 *gyejeol*

spring │ 봄 *bom*

summer │ 여름 *yeoreum*

autumn │ 가을 *gaeul*

winter │ 겨울 *gyeoul*

weather │ 날씨 *nalssi*

sunny │ 맑다 *makda*

rainy season │ 장마 *jangma*

cold │ 춥다 *chupda*

warm │ 따뜻하다 *ttatteutada*

hot │ 덥다 *deopda*

the humidity is high │ 습도가 높다 *seupdoga nopda*

cloudy │ 구름이 잔뜩 끼다 *gureumi jantteuk kkida*

hazy │ 흐리다 *heurida*

raining │ 비가 오다 *biga oda*

snowing │ 눈이 오다 *nuni oda*

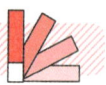

Colors

black | 검은색 *geomeunsaek*
white | 하얀색 *hayansaek*
brown | 갈색 *galsaek*
blue | 파란색 *paransaek*
green | 녹색 *noksaek*
orange | 주황색 *juhwangsaek*
gray | 회색 *hoesaek*
purple | 보라색 *borasaek*
red | 빨간색 *ppalgansaek*
yellow | 노란색 *noransaek*
pink | 분홍색 *bunhongsaek*
gold | 금색 *geumsaek*
silver | 은색 *eunsaek*
ivory | 아이보리색 *aiborisaek*

Useful Expressions

I am wearing a red sweater today.	오늘 빨간 스웨터를 입었어요. *Oneul ppalgan seuweteoreul ibeosseoyo.*
My bag is black.	제 가방은 검은색이에요. *Je gabangeun geomeunsaegieyo.*

💡 TIP

When you use a color as an adjective, like in "a red sweater," for example, leave out the syllable "색" *saek* at the end of the word. If you are talking about "a blue sky," you have to say "파란 하늘" *paran haneul* instead of "파란색 하늘" *paransaek haneul*.

Fun to Know

There are some words that are often used in Korean television programs and that you will hear a lot from your Korean friends, so they will be useful to know for daily use:

pretty | 예쁘다 *yeppeuda*

handsome | 잘생기다 *jalsaenggida*

cool | 멋있다 *meositda*

cute | 귀엽다 *gwiyeopda*

boring | 지루하다 *jiruhada*

fun | 재미있다 *jaemiitda*

> 💡 **TIP**
> Another term that is often used is "애교" *aegyo*, which refers to a cute display of affection often expressed through cute facial expressions and gestures and a babyish tone of voice. Popular examples of 애교 are the "귀요미" *gwiyomi* song and "뿌잉뿌잉" *ppuingppuing*. (Look them up!)

Slang

Young Koreans use a lot of shortened words and slang. Here are some popular words that are useful to know if you want to be able to communicate with the youngsters!

Awesome! (Jackpot!)	대박 *daebak*
oh my god	헐 *heol*
sure, I'm in	콜 *kol*
mental shock	멘붕 (멘탈 붕괴) *menbung (mental bunggoe)*
the best, extremely (when used as an adjective)	짱 *jjang*

Slang used on social media

ㅋㅋㅋㅋ	chuckling
ㅎㅎ	laughter
ㅇㅇ	yes
ㄴㄴ	no

Chapter 2

University

Korea is famous for its many universities. Therefore, Korean universities share a fierce rivalry for the top rankings. This also causes intense competition among students to get into the most prestigious universities. Many Korean high school students dream of entering one of the SKY universities. SKY is the Ivy League of Korea and refers to Seoul National University, Korea University, and Yonsei University.

Basics

university | 대학교 *daehakgyo*

graduate school | 대학원 *daehagwon*

grade, year of study | 학년 *hangnyeon*

semester | 학기 *hakgi*

lecture | 강의 *gangui*

class, lesson | 수업 *sueop*

subject | 과목 *gwamok*

major | 전공 *jeongong*

minor | 부전공 *bujeongong*

university student | 대학생 *daehaksaeng*

foreign student | 유학생 *yuhaksaeng*

exchange student | 교환학생 *gyohwan haksaeng*

bachelor's degree | 학사 *haksa*

master's degree | 석사 *seoksa*

doctorate | 박사 *baksa*

student ID card | 학생증 *haksaengjeung*

course registration | 수강신청 *sugang sincheong*

vacation | 방학 *banghak*

study | 공부하다 *gongbuhada*

teach | 가르치다 *gareuchida*

take classes | 수강하다 *suganghada*

professor | 교수님 *gyosunim*

teacher | 선생님 *seonsaengnim*

teaching assistant | 조교 *jogyo*

senior | 선배 *seonbae*

junior | 후배 *hubae*

💬 Useful Expressions

I am a university student.	저는 대학생이에요. *Jeoneun daehaksaengieyo.*
I study at Yonsei University.	연세대학교에 다녀요. *Yonseidaehakgyoe danyeoyo.*
I am a first year student.	1학년이에요. *Ilhangnyeonieyo.*
It's the course registration period.	수강신청 기간이에요. *Sugangsincheong giganieyo.*
How many classes do you take?	수업을 몇 개 들어요? *Sueobeul myeot gae deureoyo?*
I take three classes this semester.	이번 학기에는 수업을 3개 들어요. *Ibeon hakgineun sueobeul se gae deureoyo.*
How may credits do you take?	몇 학점을 들어요? *Myeot hakjeomeul deureoyo?*
I lost my student ID card.	학생증을 잃어버렸어요. *Haksaengjeungeul ireobeoryeosseoyo.*

> ### 💡 TIP
>
> **학 (學)**
>
> As you can see, a lot of school-related words contain the syllable "학" *hak*. This is the pronunciation of the Hanja (Chinese character) "學¸" which means "to learn."

Application for courses

At Korean universities the application process for courses can be similar to a lottery, and you will need a dose of luck to get into the courses you want. Always be prepared and have a list of backup courses you would like to take. There is also a strict time period in which the application process takes place. Check the dates and remind yourself to log in on time so you won't be disappointed.

Seniors and juniors

At university, students call their seniors "선배" *seonbae*, and they in turn call their juniors "후배" *hubae*. However, there is more meaning to this relationship than you might expect. 선배 are expected to take care of their 후배 by helping them with school work and even paying for their meals. In return, the 후배 is expected to reward their 선배 by assisting them with simple tasks and listening to them. The people you meet at university, and especially your 선배, can be a great help for finding a job or even a partner. So networking and sustaining good relations with your 선배 and 후배 is an important element of university life in Korea. Make sure to be good to your 선배—they can make your life a lot easier!

Facilities on Campus

campus | 캠퍼스 *kaempeoseu*
student union building | 학생회관 *haksaeng hoegwan*
lecture room | 강의실 *ganguisil*
copy room | 복사실 *boksasil*
library | 도서관 *doseogwan*
student cafeteria | 학생식당 *haksaeng sikdang*
professor's office | 연구실 *yeongusil*
bookstore | 서점 *seojeom*

Useful Expressions

Where is the library?	도서관이 어디예요? *Doseogwani eodiyeyo?*
The lecture room is on the fourth floor.	강의실은 4층에 있어요. *Ganguisireun sacheunge isseoyo.*
There is a copy room in the library.	도서관 안에 복사실이 있어요. *Doseogwan ane boksasiri isseoyo.*
Do you know where the professor is?	교수님께서 어디에 계시는지 아세요? *Gyosunimkkeseo eodie gyesineunji aseyo?*

| Where can I buy the textbook? | 교재는 어디에서 살 수 있어요?
Gyojaeneun eodieseo sal su isseoyo? |

Navigating the campus

Korean university campuses can be quite large and confusing. To make navigating easier, we recommend that you download the campus map. Be careful! The names of the buildings can be different in English and Korean. Be sure to check out both versions to avoid having to walk back over that steep hill because you went to the wrong building.

Facilities on campus

Before you go out to find things you need in the city, you should know that campuses offer a lot of different services. Of course you can find basic shops like convenience stores and stationary shops, but campuses often also offer telecom services and photo studios. So make sure to check out all the facilities!

Study spots

In Korea, there are many places where you can study comfortably and prepare for your exams. If you enjoy more quiet surroundings and are motivated by seeing others study hard, go to the library. Be aware that most seats need a reservation in advance, and during exam periods the library is packed. If you focus better with a good beat in the background, cafés are your go-to study spot! Even at night there are several spots that can help you fight off procrastination. Most libraries have at least one study room that is always open, and there are also various 24/7 study cafés near every university. Enjoy a good cup of coffee and pull that all-nighter to finish your essay. Good luck!

Majors

chemistry | 화학 *hwahak*

medicine | 의학 *uihak*

psychology | 심리학 *simnihak*

biology | 생물학 *saengmulhak*

physics | 물리학 *mullihak*

mechanical engineering | 기계공학 *gigyegonghak*

electrical engineering | 전기공학 *jeongigonghak*

architecture | 건축학 *geonchukhak*

business administration | 경영학 *gyeongyeonghak*

economics | 경제학 *gyeongjehak*

law | 법학 *beophak*

political science | 정치학 *jeongchihak*

linguistics | 언어학 *eoneohak*

literature | 문학 *munhak*

education | 교육학 *gyoyukhak*

history | 역사학 *yeoksahak*

Useful Expressions

Which field are you studying?	어떤 분야를 공부하세요? *Eotteon bunyareul gongbuhaseyo?*
What is your major?	전공이 뭐예요? *Jeongongi mwoyeyo?*
I am majoring in medicine.	저는 의학을 전공해요. *Jeoneun uihageul jeongonghaeyo.*
My minor is biology.	제 부전공은 생물학이에요. *Je bujeongongeun saengmulhagieyo.*

Studying

private lesson │ 과외 *gwaoe*

review │ 복습 *bokseup*

preparation(s) │ 예습 *yeseup*

teaching materials │ 교재 *gyojae*

book │ 책 *chaek*

dictionary │ 사전 *sajeon*

newspaper │ 신문 *sinmun*

cramming │ 벼락치기 *byeorakchigi*

take notes │ 필기하다 *pilgihada*

laptop │ 노트북 *noteubuk*

notes │ 노트 *noteu*

pencil case │ 필통 *piltong*

pencil │ 연필 *yeonpil*

pen │ 펜 *pen*

to borrow │ 빌리다 *billida*

to lend │ 빌려주다 *billyeojuda*

to copy │ 복사하다 *boksahada*

to print (out) │ 인쇄하다 *inswaehada*

Useful Expressions

Do you know where I can print?	인쇄 어디서 하는지 아세요? *Inswae eodiseo haneunji aseyo?*
Could you lend me this pen?	펜 좀 빌려주실 수 있어요? *Pen jom billyeojusil su isseoyo?*
I borrowed this book from the library.	이 책은 도서관에서 빌렸어요. *I chaegeun doseogwaneseo billyeosseoyo.*
I brought my laptop to class.	수업에 노트북을 가지고 왔어요. *Sueobe noteubugeul gajigo wasseoyo.*

Exams and Assignments

thesis │ 논문 *nonmun*

essay │ 에세이 *esei*

presentation	발표	*balpyo*
to submit, hand in	제출하다	*jechulhada*
assignment	과제	*gwaje*
question	질문	*jilmun*
deadline	마감	*magam*
grade	성적	*seongjeok*
score	점수	*jeomsu*
relative grading	상대평가	*sangdae pyeongga*
absolute grading	절대평가	*jeoldae pyeongga*
exam	시험	*siheom*
midterm examination	중간고사	*junggangosa*
final examination	기말고사	*gimalgosa*
pass	합격	*hapgyeok*
fail	불합격	*bulhapgyeok*
right	맞다	*matda*
wrong	틀리다	*teullida*
easy	쉽다	*swipda*
difficult	어렵다	*eoryeopda*

💬 Useful Expressions

Professor, when is the deadline for the essay?	교수님, 에세이 마감이 언제예요? *Gyosunim, esei magami eonjeyeyo?*
Please hand in your assignment by Thursday.	목요일까지 과제를 제출해 주세요. *Mogyoilkkaji gwajereul jechulhae juseyo.*

When is the exam?	시험은 언제예요? *Siheomeun eonjeyeyo?*
I took the exam.	시험을 봤어요. *Siheomeul bwasseoyo.*
I passed the exam!	시험에 합격했어요! *Siheome hapgyeokaesseoyo!*
I am currently writing my thesis.	지금 논문을 쓰고 있어요. *Jigeum nonmuneul sseugo isseoyo.*

Cheating

In Korea, cheating is called "컨닝" *keonning*. You can use it as a verb by adding "−하다" *hada* to the word, so "컨닝하다" means "to cheat." Another word for cheating on a test is "부정행위" *bujeonghaengwi*. You'd better bear in mind your professor's warning: "컨닝하지 마세요!" *keonninghaji maseyo*. Don't cheat!

Grading policies

Be aware that courses could have one of several grading policies, including pass/fail, absolute grading, or relative grading. Relative grading, or grading on a curve, means that your score is relative to other students in your class. For example, As are reserved for the top twenty percent of students, Bs for the next thirty percent and so on. Competition among students in these relative grading classes is very fierce, so be prepared to work hard if you take such a class!

Language Exchange and Campus Activities

foreign language | 외국어 *oegugeo*

mother tongue, native language | 모국어 *mogugeo*

second language | 제2외국어 *jeioegugeo*

English | 영어 *yeongeo*

Korean | 한국어 *hangugeo*

Chinese | 중국어 *junggugeo*

Japanese | 일본어 *ilboneo*

German | 독일어 *dogireo*

French | 프랑스어 *peurangseueo*

Spanish | 스페인어 *seupeineo*

Russian | 러시아어 *reosiaeo*

Arabic | 아랍어 *arabeo*

language exchange | 언어교환 *eoneo gyohwan*

university club | 동아리 *dongari*

membership training (MT) | 엠티 *emti*

festival | 축제 *chukje*

Useful Expressions

I am studying Korean.	저는 한국어를 공부하고 있어요. *Jeoneun hangugeoreul gongbuhago isseoyo.*
I (don't) speak Korean well.	저는 한국어를 잘(못)해요. *Jeoneun hangugeoreul jal(mot)haeyo.*

Can you speak English?	영어를 할 줄 아세요? *Yeongeoreul hal jul aseyo?*
My native language is Spanish.	제 모국어는 스페인어예요. *Je mogugeoneun seupeineoyeyo.*
I speak three languages.	저는 3개 국어를 할 수 있어요. *Jeoneun sam gae gugeoreul hal su isseoyo.*
I want to join a university club.	동아리에 지원하고 싶어요. *Dongarie jiwonhago sipeoyo.*
I am going on an MT this weekend.	이번 주말에 엠티에 갈 거예요. *Ibeon jumare emtie gal geoyeyo.*

From country to language

By adding "–어" *eo* to the name of a country, you can refer to its language. Take an example of China and Chinese: "중국" *junguk* + "어" *eo* = "중국어" *jungugeo*. This applies for countries like Japan, Korea, France, Germany, Spain, and so on. Be careful! There is no such thing as "미국어" *migugeo*, derived from "미국" *miguk* (America). All English is referred to as "영어" *yeongeo* from "영국" *yeongguk* (England).

English tutoring

Good English skills are very important in Korea, and many parents or university students are looking for a private tutor for a couple hours a week. So if you are fluent in English and are looking for a part time job, you could consider tutoring

English. If your classes are successful, there is a high chance that your services will be requested by your student's connections as well! However, make sure to check your visa conditions, since not all student visas allow part-time jobs.

Language exchange

A good way to practice your Korean is to do language exchange with a Korean student. Often, a certain student club is in charge of a mix-and-match language exchange program for which you can apply at the beginning of your semester abroad. This is also a good opportunity to make new friends! Another way is to visit one of the many language exchange cafés. Speaking time can be limited, but it is great for beginners.

University clubs

Korean universities have a lot of different clubs you can join. These clubs are called "동아리" *dongari*. There is a club for almost every hobby or interest, whether it be sports, music, photography, or making the university newspaper! At the beginning of each semester, there will be a club fair held on campus during which you can apply for the clubs you are interested in. Once you have been accepted into the club, there will likely be an MT, or membership training, organized by your club. University clubs can be very helpful when you are trying to make friends and also for making connections for your future career.

MT

MT stands for Membership Training and is a big part of student life in Korea. At an MT, people of one club or major go out of the city for at least one night to drink and have fun with their fellow students. We also participated in a MT when we attended university in Korea. It is a very unique experience during which you can meet a lot of different people, experience Korean drinking and bonding culture, and learn a lot of Korean drinking games. However, be sure to wear comfy clothes, since you will wear them all night!

University festivals

Every university in Korea holds its own music festival once a year. These festivals are organized to create a sense of brotherhood and solidarity among the students that attend that university, and they are great fun to boot!

We attended Yonsei University's festival 아카라카 (Akaraka) in 2016. The festival started with Yonsei University's school cheerleading squad, who taught the audience how to do the school cheers and the accompanying dances. It was amazing to see all the students who were attending do the school cheers at the same time, and the atmosphere of the festival was very fun and energetic. After that, there were performances by famous singers and idol groups, which ended with fireworks. Big artists such as Chang Kiha, Dok2, Lee Hi, and Twice all came to perform at the festival. If you get the chance to attend a university festival, make sure you do!

Chapter 3

Housing

It is always hard to find a place to live in a foreign country. Korea offers some unique types of housing for students, like university dormitories, boarding houses, and small one-room apartments called "고시원" *gosiwon*. Dormitories are the housing option most popular among foreign students, as students don't have to go through the trouble of finding lodging and can live close to, or even on, campus. However, be sure to check the conditions (e.g. shared rooms and facilities, rules, and prices) before applying, since they differ for every dormitory. Some dormitories offer single rooms, but in others you have to share your room with up to three other people, which is a lot cheaper. Once you have made the decision, you are stuck with it the whole semester! So take the time to consider your decision and check out the other options explained in this chapter.

Housing Types

house | 집 *jip*

gosiwon | 고시원 *gosiwon*

studio (apartment) | 원룸 *wollum*

apartment | 아파트 *apateu*

dormitory | 기숙사 *gisuksa*

boarding house | 하숙집 *hasukjip*

Useful Expressions

Where do you live?	어디 살아요? *Eodi sarayo?*
The dormitory is on campus.	기숙사는 캠퍼스에 있어요. *Gisuksaneun kaempeoseue isseoyo.*
I live in a goshiwon.	저는 고시원에 살아요. *Jeoneun gosiwone sarayo.*

Gosiwon

A well-known housing option in Korea is the "고시원" *gosiwon*. "고시" *gosi* means examination, and these small rooms were originally used by people studying for governmental exams. This is one of the cheapest forms of housing. Their size and amenities can differ a lot. There are rooms with or without windows, showers, bathrooms, refrigerators, and so on in all possible combinations, so be sure to check them out before making your decision! The advantage is that you can always switch 고시원 during your semester if you don't like it.

Boarding house

The boarding house, or "하숙집" *hasukjip*, is also an option. Here, you live in someone's home, so you can get a taste of home-cooked Korean food. Since 하숙집 are run by Korean native speakers, often middle-aged Korean women, living in a boarding house is also a good way to practice your Korean. Try to chat away in Korean over your home-cooked meals.

A studio apartment or a one-room

A studio apartment or a one-room is a small-sized apartment with monthly rent and a small deposit. It usually includes a kitchen and a bathroom, but again location, sizes, and amenities influence the deposit and rent. They are also popular among students and therefore easily found around campus areas. If you want to live in a comfortable room on your own, this could be a great option for you.

Apartments

For normal-sized apartments, deposits can make quite a dent in your savings. Although it differs per apartment, they are usually very expensive. Students often make groups of about four people and divide the deposit money. Plus, this way, you can immediately have a nice group of people to hang out with!

Housing Conditions

room rent | 방세 *bangse*

monthly rent | 월세 *wolse*

rental housing | 전세 *jeonse*

deposit | 보증금 *bojeunggeum*

contract | 계약서 *gyeyakseo*

clean | 깨끗하다 *kkaekkeutada*

dirty | 더럽다 *deoreopda*

noisy | 시끄럽다 *sikkeureopda*

quiet | 조용하다 *joyonghada*

joint, shared | 공용 *gongyong*

individual | 개인 *gaein*

women only | 여성전용 *yeoseong jeonyong*

roommate | 룸메이트 *rummeiteu*

curfew | 통행금지 (통금) *tonghaeng geumji (tonggeum)*

Useful Expressions

How much is the deposit?	보증금은 얼마예요? *Bojeunggeumeun eolmayeyo?*
I transferred the room rent.	방세를 입금했어요. *Bangsereul ipgeumhaesseoyo.*
Your monthly rent is 500,000 won.	월세는 오십만 원이에요. *Wolseneun osimman wonieyo.*

Is the kitchen shared?	공용 부엌이에요? *Gongyong bueokieyo?*
Do I have a private bathroom?	개인 화장실이 있어요? *Gaein hwajangsiri isseoyo?*
This dormitory has a curfew.	이 기숙사는 통금이 있어요. *I gisuksaneun tonggeumi isseoyo.*
This room is dirty.	방이 더러워요. *Bangi deoreowoyo.*
The room next door is noisy.	옆방이 시끄러워요. *Yeopbangi sikkeureowoyo.*

Rooms

bedroom │ 침실 *chimsil*

kitchen │ 부엌 *bueok*, 주방 *jubang*

living room │ 거실 *geosil*

study (room) │ 서재 *seojae*

bathroom │ 화장실 *hwajangsil*

shower room │ 샤워실 *syawosil*, 욕실 *yoksil*

door │ 문 *mun*

window │ 창문 *changmun*

Useful Expressions

Please open the window.	창문 열어 주세요. *Changmun yeoreo juseyo.*
Please close the door.	문 닫아 주세요. *Mun dada juseyo.*
I am in the living room!	저 지금 거실에 있어요! *Jeo jigeum geosire isseoyo!*

Bathroom etiquette

In Korea, especially in the older buildings, the toilets often clog due to weak piping. If you want to avoid the embarrassing situation of a backed-up toilet, toss your used toilet paper into the garbage bin instead.

Furniture

bed | 침대 *chimdae*

blanket | 이불 *ibul*

pillow | 베개 *begae*

wardrobe, closet | 옷장 *otjang*

bookshelf | 책장 *chaekjang*

desk | 책상 *chaeksang*

chair | 의자 *uija*

sofa, couch | 소파 *sopa*

🗨 Useful Expressions

The blanket and pillow are not included.	이불과 베개는 포함되지 않아요. *Ibulgwa begaeneun pohamdoeji anayo.*
Is there a desk in the room?	방에 책상이 있어요? *Bange chaeksangi isseoyo?*
Is there furniture in the room?	방에 가구들이 있나요? *Bange gagudeuri innayo?*

Amenities

wi-fi | 와이파이 *waipai*

(wireless) internet | (무선) 인터넷 *(museon) inteonet*

heating | 난방 *nanbang*

air conditioning | 냉방 *naengbang*

air conditioner | 에어컨 *eeokeon*

gas | 가스 *gaseu*

sink, basin | 싱크대 *singkeudae*, 세면대 *semyeondae*

bathtub | 욕조 *yokjo*

elevator | 엘리베이터 *ellibeiteo*

electricity | 전기 *jeongi*

water purifier | 정수기 *jeongsugi*

microwave | 전자레인지 *jeonjareinji*

refrigerator | 냉장고 *naengjanggo*

boiler | 보일러 *boilleo*

oven | 오븐 *obeun*

toilet | 변기 *byeongi*

shower | 샤워기 *syawogi*

washing machine | 세탁기 *setakgi*

television | 텔레비전 *tellebijeon*

📝 Useful Expressions

What is the wi-fi password?	와이파이 비밀번호가 뭐예요? *Waipai bimilbeonhoga mwoyeyo?*
The toilet is clogged.	변기가 막혔어요. *Byeongiga makyeosseoyo.*
The washing machine is not working.	세탁기가 고장났어요. *Setakgiga gojangnasseoyo.*
Please turn on the air conditioner.	에어컨을 켜 주세요. *Eeokeoneul kyeo juseyo.*
Please turn off the boiler.	보일러를 꺼 주세요. *Boilleoreul kkeo juseyo.*

Water

People in Korea usually don't drink water from the tap. Instead there are often water-purification dispensers to be found in houses, public buildings, schools, and restaurants. This might sound inconvenient, but they turn out to be quite handy. You can choose between hot and cold water, which means that you can easily find ice-cold water in the summer, and in the winter you can make tea in an instant.

Ondol

Koreans have a unique heating system called *ondol*. This heating system, which warms up the floors, has been used since ancient times. Since the winters can get really cold in Korea, the ondol is very helpful in thawing those frozen toes!

Daily Necessities

shampoo | 샴푸 *syampu*

toothbrush | 칫솔 *chitsol*

toothpaste | 치약 *chiyak*

towel | 수건 *sugeon*

mirror | 거울 *geoul*

toilet paper | 휴지 *hyuji*

detergent | 세제 *seje*

laundry detergent | 세탁용 세제 *setakyong seje*

trashcan | 쓰레기통 *sseuregitong*

light | 불 *bul*, 등 *deung*

Useful Expressions

Please throw the toilet paper into the trashcan. | 휴지는 쓰레기통에 넣어주세요. *Hyujinuen sseuregitonge neoeojuseyo.*

I am cleaning the bathroom using a cleaning agent.	세제로 화장실 청소를 하고 있어요. *Sejero hwajangsil cheongsoreul hago isseoyo.*
Please turn the light on.	불을 켜 주세요. *Bureul kyeo juseyo.*

Best places to buy living necessities

When you move into your housing of choice, you will need basic things like furniture and daily necessities. Furniture is often provided, but other practical things might be missing. In that case, Daiso (다이소) and Homeplus are then the places to be. Daiso is a chain store that offers low-priced products ranging from scissors and sticky notes to bathroom necessities and cooking supplies. If you can't find something at Daiso, then you can check out the slightly more pricey Homeplus. This is a huge supermarket offering the same goods as Daiso, but with a broader range of products. They also sell larger home supplies such as drying racks and vacuum cleaners. Along with Homeplus, other major supermarket chains include E-mart and Lotte Mart.

Chapter 4

Navigation

If you ever find yourself stranded somewhere and don't know where to go, don't worry. People are always willing to help you out even if they don't speak English well. Many cities and neighborhoods also have a tourist information center where maps are available to help you plan your stay in the area. However, the best method of finding your way in Korea is through the Naver Map app. The app is in Korean, but as long as you can type the place name in Hangeul and select it as either 도착 *dochak* (arrival) or 출발 *chulbal* (departure), you can use it to map a route.

Directions

here | 여기 *yeogi*

there | 거기 *geogi*

over there | 저기 *jeogi*

right | 오른쪽 *oreunjjok*

left | 왼쪽 *oenjjok*

neighborhood, vicinity | 근처 *geuncheo*

surroundings | 주변 *jubyeon*

area, region | 지역 *jiyeok*

neighborhood, town | 동네 *dongne*

village | 마을 *maeul*

city | 도시 *dosi*

close (to/by) | 가깝다 *gakkapda*

far (from) | 멀다 *meolda*

above, top | 위 *wi*

below, bottom | 밑 *mit*, 아래 *arae*

beside, side | 옆 *yeop*

inside | 안 *an*

front, in front of | 앞 *ap*

behind, back | 뒤 *dwi*

on the opposite side | 맞은편 *majeunpyeon*

🗨 Useful Expressions

Where is the school?	학교가 어디예요? *Hakgyoga eodiyeyo?*
The bank is on the opposite side of the street.	은행은 길 맞은편에 있어요. *Eunhaengeun gil majeunpyeone isseoyo.*
Turn right at the post office.	우체국에서 오른쪽으로 가세요. *Uchegugeseo oreunjjogeuro gaseyo.*
Is the campus far away?	캠퍼스가 여기서 멀어요? *Kaempeoseuga yeogiseo meoreoyo?*
No, it is close by.	아니요, 가까워요. *Aniyo, gakkawoyo.*
Where shall we meet?	어디서 만날까요? *Eodiseo mannalkkayo?*

On the Street

map | 지도 *jido*

street, distance | 거리 *geori*

street, route | 길 *gil*

bridge | 다리 *dari*

crosswalk | 횡단보도 *hoengdanbodo*

sidewalk | 인도 *indo*

exit | 출구 *chulgu*

entrance | 입구 *ipgu*

rush hour | 러시아워 *reosiawo*

traffic light | 신호등 *sinhodeung*

streetlight | 가로등 *garodeung*

traffic sign | 표지판 *pyojipan*

road (for cars) | 차도 *chado*

underpass | 지하도 *jihado*

highway | 고속도로 *gosokdoro*

intersection | 사거리 *sageori*

traffic is backed up | 길이 막히다 *giri makida*

traffic jam | 교통 체증 *gyotong chejeung*

bank | 은행 *eunhang*

post office | 우체국 *ucheguk*

church | 교회 *gyohoe*

park | 공원 *gongwon*

Useful Expressions

You should turn left at the bank.	은행에서 왼쪽으로 꺾으시면 돼요. *Eunhaengeseo oenjjogeuro kkeokkeusimyeon dwaeyo.*
Cross the bridge and walk on the sidewalk.	다리를 건너서 인도로 걸어가세요. *Darireul geonneoseo indoro georeogaseyo.*
It is rush hour, so traffic is backed up.	러시아워라서 길이 막혀요. *Reosiaworaseo giri makyeoyo.*

How long does it take to get from here to the subway station?	여기서 지하철역까지 얼마나 걸려요? *Yeogiseo jihacheollyeokkkaji eolmana geollyeoyo?*
Turn right at the next intersection.	다음 사거리에서 오른쪽으로 가세요. *Daeum sageorieseo oreunjjogeuro gaseyo.*

Traffic signs

Most traffic signs are universal, but we spotted a few interesting ones in Korea. Many Koreans have a habit of walking and looking at their mobile phone at the same time. This has caused accidents, so in response Korea has created a unique sign prohibiting the use of cell phones while crossing the crosswalk. Another interesting sign is the sticker found in taxis warning customers to watch out for motorcycles when they get in and out of the taxi. In Korea, there is a massive amount of delivery bikes swirling around traffic as fast as possible. Keep an eye out for them so you don't get hit!

Transportation

transportation │ 교통 *gyotong*

public transportation │ 대중교통 *daejung gyotong*

car │ 자동차 *jadongcha*

bus │ 버스 *beoseu*

taxi │ 택시 *taeksi*

airplane │ 비행기 *bihaenggi*

subway │ 지하철 *jihacheol*

train │ 기차 *gicha*

bicycle │ 자전거 *jajeongeo*

subway line │ 호선 *hoseon*

transfer │ 환승 *hwanseung*

platform │ 승강장 *seunggangjang*

schedule │ 시간표 *siganpyo*

parking lot │ 주차장 *juchajang*

bus stop │ 버스 정류장 *beoseu jeongnyujang*

taxi stand │ 택시 승차장 *taeksi seungchajang*

airport │ 공항 *gonghang*

station │ 역 *yeok*

driver │ 운전기사 *unjeongisa*

driver's license │ 운전면허 *unjeonmyeonheo*

Useful Expressions

Which platform does the train leave from?	기차가 어느 승강장에서 출발해요? *Gichaga eoneu seunggangjangeseo chulbalhaeyo?*
I need to call a taxi.	택시를 불러야겠어요. *Taeksireul bulleoyagesseoyo.*
Please drive/go to Seoul Station.	서울역으로 가 주세요. *Seouryeogeuro ga juseyo.*

Which subway line should I take?

지하철 몇 호선을 타면 돼요?
Jihacheol myeot hoseoneul tamyeon dwaeyo?

Subway

The subway is one of the main means of transportation in the major cities. There are several great subway apps available to guide you, and you can easily follow the signs at the stations.

In the subway, it is recommdended to not sit on the seats reserved for the elderly, pregnant women, children, or injured passengers, even when all the other seats are taken. There are also pink seats reserved for pregnant women or women with babies. Be warned, the subway has acquired the nickname "지옥철" *jiokcheol*, meaning "subway from hell," thanks to the overwhelming number of passengers on certain lines during rush hour.

Taxis

In Korea, particularly Seoul, taxis are everywhere, and at quite a reasonable cost, you can travel anywhere. There are several types of taxis. The regular taxis in Seoul are orange, white, or silver and charge the lowest fare, usually starting from KRW 3,000 and increasing as you go. Be sure to check whether the taxi driver turns on the meter. You can ask, "미터를 켜 주세요" *Miteoreul kyeo juseyo*. (Please turn on the meter.) The black taxis, which have a "모범" *mobeom* sign on the roof, are luxury taxis with a higher fare. To catch a taxi, you can just wave your hand on the street, wait at a taxi stand, or call a cab, either by telephone or by app. Finally, don't forget that buses and subways finish operation earlier on the weekends, and only night cabs, which charge a slightly higher fee, are available after that.

Taxi drivers

Taking a taxi is a great chance to practice your Korean. Taxi drivers frequently like to chat with customers, and if you utter just a few Korean words, they won't hesitate to speak to you. Taxi drivers like to take on the role of teacher, tour guide, or politician. Getting a long, critical speech about the inefficiency of the Korean government is common. These rides can certainly be very interesting!

Buses

Buses are a convenient means of transport in Korea. To pay for a bus ride, simply tap your T-money card on the machine when getting on and off the bus. Aside from a large number of normal city buses, there are several specialized buses. To travel from the airport to nearby areas, you can take the airport limousine bus for somewhere between KRW 10,000 and 15,000. To travel between cities, the express bus, called "고속버스" *gosokbeoseu*, is highly recommended as a cheaper alternative to the train. To prevent waiting for hours on weekends or holidays, we recommend that you buy the tickets in advance.

Verbs

to drive | 운전하다 *unjeonhada*

to make a U-turn | 유턴하다 *yuteonhada*

to turn left | 좌회전하다 *jwahoejeonhada*

to turn right | 우회전하다 *uhoejeonhada*

to transfer | 갈아타다 *garatada*, 환승하다 *hwanseunghada*

to stop (car, taxi) | 세우다 *seuda*

to get on/into (a vehicle) | 타다 *tada*

to get off/out of (a vehicle) | 내리다 *naerida*

to depart | 출발하다 *chulbalhada*

to arrive | 도착하다 *dochakhada*

to go | 가다 *gada*

to come | 오다 *oda*

Useful Expressions

Where do I need to get off?	어디서 내려야 해요? *Eodiseo naeryeoya haeyo?*
You can get on at Gangnam station.	강남역에서 타시면 돼요. *Gangnamyeogeseo tasimyeon dwaeyo.*
I am getting on at this station.	이번 역에서 탈 거예요. *Ibeon yeogeseo tal geoyeyo.*
Do I need to transfer?	환승해야 돼요? *Hwanseunghaeya dwaeyo?*

You can transfer to Line 1 at Seoul Station.	서울역에서 1호선으로 갈아탈 수 있어요. *Seoulyeogeseo ilhoseoneuro garatal su isseoyo.*
Please stop here.	여기서 세워 주세요. *Yeogiseo sewo juseyo.*
How do I get to the post office?	우체국에 어떻게 가요? *Ucheguge eotteoke gayo?*
Make a U-turn over there.	저기서 유턴하세요. *Jeogiseo yuteonhaseyo.*

💡 TIP

If you want to say "I am going by … (a form of transportation)" in Korean, you usually use the phrase "____로 갈 거예요" *ro gal geoyeyo*. You can fill in the blank with any type of transportation, except "foot," which has its own unique phrase. See the difference:

I am going by foot.	걸어서 갈 거예요. *Georeoseo gal geoyeyo.*
I am going by train.	기차로 갈 거예요. *Gicharo gal geoyeyo.*

Tickets

ticket | 티켓 *tiket*, 표 *pyo*
ticket office | 매표소 *maepyoso*
ticket machine | 티켓 발매기 *tiket balmaegi*
one-way | 편도 *pyeondo*
round-trip | 왕복 *wangbok*
fee | 요금 *yogeum*
transportation cost | 교통비 *gyotongbi*
transportation card | 교통카드 *gyotongkadeu*
to charge | 충전하다 *chungjeonhada*
to reserve | 예약하다 *yeyakhada*

Useful Expressions

I would like one ticket from Seoul to Jeonju, please.	서울에서 전주 가는 티켓 한 장 주세요. *Seouleseo jeonju ganeun tiket han jang juseyo.*
A round-trip ticket from Seoul to Daegu please.	서울에서 대구로 가는 왕복 티켓 주세요. *Seouleseo daeguro ganeun wangbok tiket juseyo.*
Please charge my T-money card with 10,000 won.	티머니카드에 만 원 충전해 주세요. *Timeonikadeue man won chungjeonhae juseyo.*

Which bus goes to Busan?	어느 버스가 부산으로 가요? *Eoneu beoseuga busaneuro gayo?*
When does the next train leave?	다음 기차는 언제 출발해요? *Daeum gichaneun eonje chulbalhaeyo?*
How much is one ticket?	티켓 한 장에 얼마예요? *Tiket han jange eolmayeyo?*
How long does the train take from Seoul to Busan?	서울에서 부산까지 기차로 몇 시간 걸려요? *Seoureseo busankkaji gicharo myeot sigan geollyeoyo?*

T-money card

A T-money card makes public transport very easy. The bus, subway, and even taxis can be paid with this card. The card can be bought at all convenience stores and comes in many different designs, including those with photos of your favorite K-pop group. You can charge them at the subway stations or any convenience store. At the end of your stay, you can reclaim the money that is left on your card at those same places.

Chapter 5

Food

The student cafeteria on your university campus is a place where you will most likely eat quite often during your stay in Korea. It is cheap, fast, and perfect for meals between classes. The menu usually includes staple dishes from the Korean, Japanese, Chinese, and Western kitchen. In other cases, cafeterias choose to offer only a select few dishes, which change every day. To order a dish, you usually order your dish with the front cashier and get a receipt with a number on it. When your food is ready, the number will appear on a screen, and you can go pick up your tray from the designated kitchen counter.

Places and Service

restaurant | 식당 *sikdang*

café | 카페 *kape*

good place to eat | 맛집 *matjip*

convenience store | 편의점 *pyeonuijeom*

unlimited refill | 무한리필 *muhanripil*

self-serve | 셀프 *selpeu*

addition | 추가 *chuga*

on the house | 서비스 *seobiseu*

📝 Useful Expressions

I drank coffee at a café.	카페에서 커피를 마셨어요. *Kapeeseo keopireul masyeosseoyo.*
I bought *gimbap* at the convenience store.	편의점에서 김밥을 샀어요. *Pyeonuijeomeseo gimbabeul sasseoyo.*
The side dishes are self-serve.	반찬은 셀프예요. *Banchaneun selpeuyeyo.*
You can get unlimited refills on your cola here.	여기는 콜라를 무한리필할 수 있어요. *Yeogineun kollareul muhanripilhal su isseoyo.*
The coffee is on the house.	커피는 서비스예요. *Keopineun seobiseuyeyo.*

Good restaurants

In Korea, people often go out for dinner, and there are a lot of good restaurants. Plenty of restaurants are open late at night, and most convenience stores are 24/7, so you'll never go hungry in Korea. However, to find the hidden gems and the most amazing dishes, ask for recommendations from a Korean friend or look for reviews on Naver. The popular restaurants that serve delicious dishes for good prices are called "맛집" *matjip*. However, in Korea, food trends change quickly, and restaurants come and go in the blink of an eye. To make sure you get a taste of all the best food Korea has to offer, make check out all the 맛집, but don't wait too long, or the restaurants may be gone!

Service

In Korean restaurants, water is usually brought to you in a carafe or bottle with accompanying cups, or it may be self-serve. In case of the latter, there will be a water purifier and cups for your use. You can usually also refill side dishes, such as kimchi or radish, for free. Extra ingredients, sauces, or small side dishes that can be added onto your order for a small fee are labeled on the menu under "추가" *chuga*. When you become a regular customer, restaurants will sometimes give you something on the house, which is called "서비스" *seobiseu*.

Ordering and Paying

order | 주문 *jumun*

menu | 메뉴 *menyu*

portion | 인분 *inbun*

delivery | 배달 *baedal*

take-out | 포장 *pojang*

free | 무료 *muryo*

separately | 각자 *gakja*

to pay | 계산하다 *gyesanhada*

going Dutch | 더치페이 *deochipei*

receipt | 영수증 *yeongsujeung*

💬 Useful Expressions

What you can say:

I would like to order.	주문할게요. *Jumunhalgeyo.*
I would like take-out, please.	포장해 주세요. *Pojanghae juseyo.*
How long do we have to wait?	얼마나 기다려야 해요? *Eolmana gidaryeoya haeyo?*
Do you have a menu in English?	영어로 된 메뉴판 있어요? *Yeongeoro doen menyupan isseoyo?*
We would like to pay separately.	각자 계산할게요. *Gakja gyesanhalgeyo.*

What you might hear:

May I take your order?	주문하시겠어요? *Jumunhasigesseoyo?*
Will you be eating here?	드시고 가세요? *Deusigo gaseyo?*
May I wrap this for you?	포장해 드릴까요? *Pojanghae deurilkkayo?*
How many people (in your party)?	몇 분이세요? *Myeot buniseyo?*
Would you like a receipt?	영수증 드릴까요? *Yeongsujeung deurilkkayo?*

How to order

Ordering in a Korean restaurant can be quite challenging. In some restaurants there is only a big menu on the wall, and often there is no English menu. There are two ways to order. In a lot of restaurants, the tables come with a bell you can press to get the attention of the staff. A waiter will then come to your table to take your order or assist you. If there is no bell, you have to signal to the waiters. However, closing the menu or waving your hand is not enough. You have to raise your voice and call out either "주문할게요" *jumunhalgeyo* (I am ready to order) or "저기요" *jeogiyo* (a call for attention). This is in no way considered rude or impatient, so don't be shy!

Going Dutch

When you have ordered, in some restaurants you immediately get the receipt for your table. When you are done eating, you take this receipt to the register. In Korea, you don't have to pay tip.

It has long been a custom in Korea that elders pay for the younger people when eating or drinking something together. However, more and more people, particularly young students, now use "더치페이" *deochipei*, otherwise known as "going Dutch," instead. At the counter, the amount will be split evenly, or you can pay for the dish you ate.

Eating

eating out | 외식 *oesik*

to cook | 요리하다 *yorihada*

to set the table | 상을 차리다 *sangeul charida*

to do grocery shopping | 장보다 *jangboda*

to be full | 배부르다 *baebureuda*

to be hungry | 배고프다 *baegopeuda*

to eat | 먹다 *meokda*

meal | 식사 *siksa*

breakfast | 아침 *achim*

lunch | 점심 *jeomsim*

dinner | 저녁 *jeonyeok*

eating alone | 혼밥 *honbap*

Useful Expressions

Bon appétit.	잘 먹겠습니다. *Jal meokgetseumnida.*
I enjoyed my meal.	잘 먹었어요. *Jal meogeosseoyo.*
Have you eaten dinner?	저녁 먹었어요? *Jeonyeok meogeosseoyo?*
I'm hungry!	배고파요! *Baegopayo!*

Eating alone

Eating out alone, called "혼밥" *honbap*, can be difficult when a restaurant only offers multi-person dishes, but Korea is getting used to providing single servings. Many restaurants offer single-person tables. If you are busy but don't want to have takeout in your room, don't hesitate to try out a restaurant on your own.

> **TIP**
>
> 아침 *achim* (breakfast) and 저녁 *jeonyeok* (dinner) not only refer to specific meals, but also to the corresponding time of the day.

Flavors

taste | 맛 *mat*
salty | 짜다 *jjada*
sweet | 달다 *dalda*
bitter | 쓰다 *sseuda*
sour | 시다 *sida*
mild | 순하다 *sunhada*
spicy | 맵다 *maepda*
bland | 싱겁다 *singgeopda*
delicious | 맛있다 *masitda*
not good tasting | 맛없다 *madeopda*
greasy | 느끼하다 *neukkihada*
strong | 자극적이다 *jageukjeogida*

Useful Expressions

How does it taste?	맛이 어때요? *Masi eottaeyo?*
It is very delicious!	아주 맛있어요! *Aju masisseoyo.*
It's too spicy!	너무 매워요! *Neomu maewoyo!*

> **💡 TIP**
>
> Be aware, Korean food can be quite spicy, and they don't have milk in the restaurant to cool your mouth. If you are sensitive to spicy food, you can say:
>
> | Please make it less spicy. | 덜 맵게 해 주세요. *Deol maepge hae juseyo.* |
> | --- | --- |
> | I would like the mild version, please. | 순한 맛으로 주세요. *Sunhan maseuro juseyo.* |

Drinking

to be thirsty │ 목이 마르다 *mogi mareuda*

to drink │ 마시다 *masida*

water │ 물 *mul*

mineral water │ 생수 *saengsu*

milk │ 우유 *uyu*

juice │ 주스 *juseu*

tea │ 차 *cha*

beverage │ 음료(수) *eumnyo(su)*

(iced) coffee │ (아이스) 커피 *(aiseu) keopi*

liquor │ 술 *sul*

soju │ 소주 *soju*

beer | 맥주 *maekju*

makgeolli | 막걸리 *makgeolli*

wine | 와인 *wain*

💬 Useful Expressions

I drink tea.	저는 차를 마셔요. *Jeoneun chareul masyeoyo.*
I am thirsty.	목이 말라요. *Mogi mallayo.*
Please give me a cup of hot coffee.	따뜻한 커피 한 잔 주세요. *ttatteutan keopi han jan juseyo.*
I don't drink alcohol.	저는 술을 마시지 않아요. *Jeoneun sureul masiji anhayo.*

Soju and makgeolli

소주 *soju* and 막걸리 *makgeolli* are Korean liquors. 소주 is a clear alcoholic drink with an alcohol percentage of around 20 percent. These days, they also offer soju in different fruit flavors. It is very popular among Koreans and very cheap. 막걸리 is a creamy-colored Korean alcoholic drink made from rice. It has 6-8 percent alcohol and is traditionally drunk from a bowl. Since it is a nutritious drink and is currently offered in many different flavors, you have a good excuse to give it a shot!

Ingredients

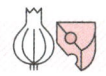

ingredients | 재료 *jaeryo*

kimchi | 김치 *gimchi*

meat | 고기 *gogi*

pork | 돼지고기 *dwaejigogi*

beef | 소고기 *sogogi*

ham | 햄 *haem*

fish | 생선 *saengseon*

soybean paste | 된장 *doenjang*

soy sauce | 간장 *ganjang*

red pepper paste | 고추장 *gochujang*

salt | 소금 *sogeum*

sugar | 설탕 *seoltang*

vinegar | 식초 *sikcho*

octopus | 문어 *muneo*

small octopus | 낙지 *nakji*

squid | 오징어 *ojingeo*

shrimp | 새우 *saeu*

potato | 감자 *gamja*

tofu | 두부 *dubu*

seaweed | 미역 *miyeok*

onion | 양파 *yangpa*

garlic | 마늘 *maneul*

egg | 계란 *gyeran*

cheese | 치즈 *chijeu*

vegetables | 야채 *yachae*

lettuce | 상추 *sangchu*

💬 Useful Expressions

I don't like tofu.	저는 두부를 싫어해요. *Jeoneun dubureul sireohaeyo.*
Is there red pepper paste in this dish?	이 요리에 고추장이 들어가요? *I yorie gochujangi deureogayo?*
Please add a little salt.	소금을 조금 넣어주세요. *Sogeumeul jogeum neoeojuseyo.*
Please take out the garlic.	마늘은 빼 주세요. *Maneureun ppae juseyo.*
Please give me more lettuce.	상추 조금만 더 주세요. *Sangchu jogeumman deo juseyo.*
Is this a meat dish?	이건 고기 요리예요? *Igeon gogi yorieyo?*

Dishes and Fruit

cooking, dishes | 요리 *yori*

side dish | 반찬 *banchan*

pork belly | 삼겹살 *samgyeopsal*

bulgogi (grilled marinated beef) | 불고기 *bulgogi*

bean paste stew | 된장찌개 *doenjang jjigae*

soft tofu stew | 순두부찌개 *sundubu jjigae*

braised spicy chicken with vegetables | 찜닭 *jjimdak*

chicken | 치킨 *chikin*

chicken and beer | 치맥 *chimaek*

soup | 국 *guk*

noodles | 국수 *guksu*

instant noodles | 라면 *ramyeon*

fruit | 과일 *gwail*

apple | 사과 *sagwa*

banana | 바나나 *banana*

tangerine | 귤 *gyul*

watermelon | 수박 *subak*

strawberry | 딸기 *ttalgi*

bowl of rice | 공기밥 *gonggibap*

fried rice | 볶음밥 *bokkeumbap*

gimbap (dried seaweed rolls) | 김밥 *gimbap*

bibimbap (rice mixed with vegetables and beef) | 비빔밥 *bibimbap*

porridge | 죽 *juk*

stir-fried rice cake | 떡볶이 *tteokbokki*

fried food | 튀김 *twigim*

green-onion pancake | 파전 *pajeon*

bread | 빵 *ppang*

salad | 샐러드 *saelleodeu*

shaved ice with syrup | 빙수 *bingsu*

ice cream | 아이스크림 *aiseukeurim*

💬 Useful Expressions

Please give me three portions of *jjimdak*.	찜닭 3인분 주세요. *Jjimdak saminbun juseyo.*
Please give me four bowls of rice.	공기밥 네 개 주세요. *Gonggibap ne gae juseyo.*
How do I eat this?	이건 어떻게 먹어요? *Igeon eotteoke meogeoyo?*
My favorite food is fried rice.	제가 제일 좋아하는 음식은 볶음밥이에요. *Jega jeil joahaneun eumsigeun bokkeumbabieyo.*

💡 TIP

In Korean, the name of a country's cuisine is often made out of a combination of the country name and the word for food, "음식" *eumsik*. For example, 한국 *hanguk* (Korea) + 음식 becomes "한식" *hansik*, meaning Korean food. Therefore:

Korean food	한식 *hansik*
Japanese food	일식 *ilsik*
Chinese food	중식 *jungsik*
Western food	양식 *yangsik*

Street food

You can spot many street food stands in Korea. The Myeongdong (명동) area is especially famous for delicious street food. The stalls offer various kinds of food, snacks and drinks for a low price. You can also find these various street food dishes at local markets. A popular one in Seoul is Gwangjang Sijang (광장시장) in the Jongno (종로) area. We highly recommend at least one visit. If you are hungry, take a look and discover the many different flavors that the Korean streets have to offer!

Food challenges

Korea offers its fair share of unique-tasting dishes, such as fermented stingray and live octopus. We recommend that you try many; you may be surprised! We once entered a nice looking barbecue restaurant in in Andong (안동). It was very similar to a place we had previously eaten 삼겹살 *samgyeopsal* (pork belly). However, the menu inside showed that this restaurant was for intestine, which you might not eat very often back at home. The waiter helped pick out dishes that would be interesting to try, and, in the end, it was a delicious meal!

Kimchi addiction

There is one famous dish that you might have heard of, or tasted, before coming to Korea: kimchi! Vegetables, usually cabbage, are seasoned with various ingredients and then fermented to achieve this super healthy side dish that you can find on almost every Korean table. Although we didn't enjoy kimchi very much at first, we fell in love with the dish after a while. We were able to differentiate between fresh kimchi and the delicate long-fermented kimchi, which is called "묵은지" *mugeunji*, and we even visited restaurants known for their delicious kimchi. We are proud to be able to say that we have become kimchi experts!

> ### 💡 TIP
>
> If you cannot eat certain kinds of food, you can use the following sentences in restaurants.
>
> | | |
> |---|---|
> | I am vegetarian. | 저는 채식주의자예요.
Jeoneun chaesikjuuijayeyo. |
> | I can't eat meat. | 저는 고기를 못 먹어요.
Jeoneun gogireul mot meogeoyo. |
> | I am allergic to fish. | 저는 생선에 알레르기가 있어요.
Jeoneun saengseone allereugiga isseoyo. |
> | Do you have halal food? | 할랄 음식 있어요?
Hallal eumsik isseoyo? |

Tableware

bowl | 그릇 *geureut*

plate | 접시 *jeopsi*

stone pot | 돌솥 *dolsot*

grill | 불판 *bulpan*

(a pair of) chopsticks | 젓가락 *jeotgarak*

spoon | 숟가락 *sutgarak*

fork | 포크 *pokeu*

knife | 칼 *kal*, 나이프 *naipeu*

apron | 앞치마 *apchima*

bottle | 병 *byeong*

glass | 잔 *jan*

cup | 컵 *keop*

Useful Expressions

Please change the grill.	불판 바꿔 주세요. *Bulpan bakkwo juseyo.*
We need one more cup, please.	컵 하나 더 주세요. *Keop hana deo juseyo.*
Would you please bring me an apron?	앞치마 가져다 주시겠어요? *Apchima gajyeoda jusigesseoyo?*

Chapter 6

Leisure Activities

When you arrive in Korea, of course the first thing you want to do is go sightseeing! Korea has a lot of beautiful ancient buildings and nature for you to enjoy. The government has an official website, english.visitkorea.or.kr, which gives advice about the best places to visit and interesting events. They also have a convenient app for your smartphone.

Having Fun

TV drama | 드라마 *deurama*

variety show | 예능 *yeneung*

play | 연극 *yeonguek*

movie | 영화 *yeonghwa*

theater | 영화관 *yeonghwagwan*, 극장 *geukjang*

subtitles | 자막 *jamak*

reading books | 독서 *dokseo*

musical | 뮤지컬 *myujikeol*

Korean sauna | 찜질방 *jjimjilbang*

amusement park | 놀이공원 *norigongwon*

internet café | PC방 *pissibang*

Useful Expressions

What is your hobby?	취미가 뭐예요? *Chwimiga mwoyeyo?*
I like watching TV dramas.	저는 드라마 보는 걸 좋아해요. *Jeoneun deurama boneun geol joahaeyo.*
How much is a play ticket?	연극 티켓은 얼마예요? *Yeongeuk tikeseun eolmayeyo?*
I watched that movie in the theater.	그 영화는 영화관에서 봤어요. *Geu yeonghwaneun yeonghwaguaneseo bwasseoyo.*

That TV show is a lot of fun!	그 예능은 정말 재미있어요! *Geu yeneungeun jeongmal jaemiisseoyo!*
I went to the amusement park yesterday.	어제 놀이공원에 갔어요. *Eoje norigongwone gasseoyo.*
I would like to reserve three musical tickets.	뮤지컬 티켓 세 장 예약할게요. *Myujikeol tiket se jang yeyakhalgeyo.*

Room culture

In Korea, there are a lot of facilities that end with the suffix "방" *bang* (room), such as 노래방 *noraebang* (karaoke rooms) and PC방 *pissibang* (internet cafés). This is because you literally get your own room where you can have fun to your heart's content. Other examples of 방 are the DVD방, where you can rent a room to watch DVDs, and the 멀티방 *meoltibang*, where you can play games, sing karaoke, and watch movies!

Themed cafés

In Korea, the streets are bursting with cafés. Because of this café overload, Koreans have developed a fantastic phenomenon: 테마 카페 *tema kape* (themed cafés). Whether you like dogs, cats, dressing up, Hello Kitty, playing board games, or making puzzles, there is a themed café for pretty much everything. Make sure to check out what kind of cafés there are in your neighborhood!

MUSIC

music | 음악 *eumak*

to listen | 듣다 *deutta*

to sing a song | 노래를 부르다 *noraereul bureuda*

radio | 라디오 *radio*

concert | 콘서트 *konseoteu*

street performance | 거리 공연 *geori gongyeon*

karaoke | 노래방 *noraebang*

musical instrument | 악기 *akgi*

to play (musical instrument) | 연주하다 *yeonjuhada*

guitar | 기타 *gita*

piano | 피아노 *piano*

violin | 바이올린 *baiollin*

Useful Expressions

I have heard that song!	그 노래 들어봤어요! *Geu norae deureobwasseoyo!*
My hobby is going to karaoke.	제 취미는 노래방에 가는 거예요. *Je chwimineun noraebange ganeun geoyeyo.*
How was the concert yesterday night?	어젯밤 콘서트는 어땠어요? *Eojetbam konseoteuneun eottaesseoyo?*
I play the guitar.	저는 기타를 쳐요. *Jeoneun gitareul chyeoyo.*

Street performances

A lot of Korean people that dream of being a singer or a dancer perform on the street to get more recognition. These busking performances especially happen a lot in university districts such as Hongdae (홍대) and Sinchon (신촌). Street performers can usually be found at the same time and place every week. We lived in Sinchon for a year, and there we regularly saw the same buskers performing each week. Street performances range from solo singers to bands, and from idol group dances to breakdancing. Make sure to check them out when you are outside and not in a hurry!

SPORTS

sports | 스포츠 *seupocheu*

to exercise | 운동하다 *undonghada*

basketball | 농구 *nonggu*

baseball | 야구 *yagu*

soccer | 축구 *chukgu*

ball | 공 *gong*

table tennis | 탁구 *takgu*

swimming | 수영 *suyeong*

jogging | 조깅 *joging*

skiing | 스키 *seuki*

(ice) skating | (아이스) 스케이트 *(aiseu) seukeiteu*

taekwondo | 태권도 *taekwondo*

badminton | 배드민턴 *baedeuminteon*

tennis | 테니스 *teniseu*

game | 게임 *geim*, 경기 *gyeonggi*

gym | 헬스장 *helseujang*

💡 TIP

If you want to say you play a sport, you use one of several verbs:

to do, play	하다 *hada*	basketball, baseball, soccer, swimming, taekwondo
to ride	타다 *tada*	skiing, (ice) skating, biking
to play	치다 *chida*	badminton, tennis, table tennis

💬 Useful Expressions

I have never been to a baseball game.	저는 야구 경기에 가본 적이 없어요. *Jeoneun yagu gyeongie gabon jeogi eopseoyo.*
I play basketball every week.	저는 매주 농구를 해요. *Jeoneun maeju nonggureul haeyo.*
I like skiing.	스키 타는 것을 좋아해요. *Seuki taneun geoseul joahaeyo.*
I play tennis every week.	저는 매주 테니스를 쳐요. *Jeoneun maeju teniseureul chyeoyo.*

Sports cheering

In Korea, going to sports games is not just about the sports, but also about the cheering! Each Korean sports team has their own cheering team, an 응원단 *eungwondan*, and each sports team uses different songs and dances for their cheers. This makes for a very festive and enthusiastic atmosphere, and we wholeheartedly recommend you visit a Korean sports game.

Gym

Korean university campuses are very large and contain a lot of facilities. One of those facilities is a gym, for which a membership is usually cheaper than at off-campus gyms. If you like to work up a sweat, check out your university campus gym facilities first.

SIGHTSEEING AND OUTDOOR ACTIVITIES

culture | 문화 *munhwa*
(to go) sightseeing | 관광(하다) *gwangwang(hada)*
tourist information center | 관광 안내소 *gwangwang annaeso*
tourist | 관광객 *gwangwanggaek*
entrance ticket | 입장권 *ipjanggwon*
museum | 박물관 *bangmulgwan*
Buddhist temple | 사찰 *sachal*, 절 *jeol*
palace | 궁궐 *gunggwol*
to stroll | 산책하다 *sanchaekhada*
to hike | 등산하다 *deungsanhada*

river | 강 *gang*

mountain | 산 *san*

beach | 해변 *haebyeon*

sea | 바다 *bada*

backpacking | 배낭여행 *baenangyeohaeng*

camping | 캠핑 *kaemping*

💬 Useful Expressions

Two entrance tickets to Gyeongbokgung Palace, please.	경복궁 입장권 두 장 주세요. *Gyeongbokgung ipjanggwon du jang juseyo.*
I am backpacking through Korea.	저는 한국에서 배낭여행을 하는 중이에요. *Jeoneun hangugeseo baenangyeohaengeul haneun jungieyo.*
I went hiking on the mountain.	등산을 갔어요. *Deungsaneul gasseoyo.*
I went camping next to the river.	강 옆에서 캠핑을 했어요. *Gang yeopeseo kaempingeul haesseoyo.*

The Korean Wave

The Korean Wave is the increase in global popularity of South Korean culture since the 1990s. Korean dramas and Korean popular music (K-pop) have become increasingly popular all around the world, which has led to more and more foreign people gaining interest in Korean culture and a sharp increase in the amount of tourists visiting South Korea. In Korea, many companies use Korean actors and idols as their advertising models. Celebrities even advertise products such as noodles and smartphones!

Nightlife

Fire Friday | 불금 *bulgeum*

club | 클럽 *keulleop*

to dance | 춤추다 *chumchuda*

to have a party | 파티를 하다 *patireul hada*

round two | 2차 *icha*

bar | 술집 *suljip*

beer mixed with soju | 소맥 *somaek*

cocktail | 칵테일 *kakteil*

one shot | 원샷 *wonsyat*

cheers | 건배 *geonbae*

to get drunk | 취하다 *chwihada*

to have a drink | 한 잔 하다 *han jan hada*

Useful Expressions

Do you have time on Friday?	금요일에 시간 있어요? *Geumyoile sigan isseoyo?*
Would you have a drink?	한 잔 할래요? *Han jan hallaeyo?*

Let's go to karaoke for round two!	2차로 노래방에 가요! *Icharo noraebange gayo!*
I feel like I'm drunk.	취한 것 같아요. *Chwihan geot gatayo.*

Fire Friday

In Korea, Friday is the day when everyone goes out and has fun. The day has a nickname, "불금" *bulgeum* (Fire Friday), which is short for "불타는 금요일" *bultaneun geumyoil* (Burning Friday)! The expression is similar to TGIF (Thank God It's Friday).

The legal drinking age for Koreans is 19 years old in Western age. When Koreans go drinking, they often go for different "rounds" called 1차 *ilcha*, 2차 *icha*, 3차 *samcha*, etc. In every round, the whole group goes to a different place, such as a pub, a club, or a karaoke room. The best districts in Seoul to go to if you're looking for a party are Hongdae (홍대), Itaewon (이태원), and Gangnam (강남). Most college students and people in their 20s go to Hongdae, while many foreigners and Koreans looking for a Western-style party go to Itaewon. Gangnam is a little more posh, so going out there can be more expensive than in the other two districts. If you want to experience the wild side of Korea, go out and unleash your inner party animal!

Korean drinking culture

Drinking is a very popular pastime, especially on Fire Friday! However, when drinking with Koreans, you have to be careful to stick to Korean drinking etiquette. First, make sure not to pour your own drink, but let other people pour your drink for you. Koreans will refill your glass whenever they see it is empty, so if you don't want constant refills, keep your drink half full. Second, if you are drinking with superiors, such as 선배 *seonbae* or elders, always turn your head away while you drink. Facing a superior while drinking is considered impolite. Also, make sure to use two hands when you pour a drink for your superiors or accept a drink from them. This is especially important at 회식 *hoesik* (company get-togethers), when you go out and drink copious amounts of alcohol with your colleagues. At a 회식, it is deemed somewhat impolite to refuse a drink from a superior, and it's better to drink what is offered to you. If you are planning to drink with Koreans, make sure you know these rules by heart!

Types of drinking spots

There are several different types of bars in Korea. One of the most popular drinking spots are 포장마차 *pojangmacha*, which are street stalls where you can buy a variety of popular street foods along with basic alcoholic drinks like beer and soju. These days, there are also a lot of restaurants that call themselves 포장마차 and only serve alcohol and food to go with it.

Another drinking spot that you might want to try are 막걸리 *makgeolli* bars. Usually, these types of bars have a traditional interior and serve different types of makgeolli, such as banana makgeolli and chestnut makgeolli. We recommend that you try drinking makgeolli while eating some 파전 *pajeon* (green onion pancakes). It is an extremely delicious combination!

There are also a lot of Western-style bars in Seoul. These can mostly be found in the Hongdae and Itaewon districts. The Western-style bars in Seoul often have games such as beer pong and darts.

Dating

to date │ 데이트하다 *deiteuhada*

to have a casual dating relationship │ 썸타다 *sseomtada*

to go out │ 사귀다 *sagwida*

college sweethearts │ 캠퍼스 커플 (CC) *kaempeoseu keopeul*

date │ 데이트 *deiteu*

group blind date	미팅 *miting*
blind date	소개팅 *sogaeting*
to break up	헤어지다 *heeojida*
guy friend	남자 사람 친구 (남사친) *namja saram chingu (namsachin)*
woman friend	여자 사람 친구 (여사친) *yeoja saram chingu (yeosachin)*
boyfriend	남자친구 (남친) *namjachingu (namchin)*
girlfriend	여자친구 (여친) *yeojachingu (yeochin)*

💬 Useful Expressions

Do you have a boyfriend?	남자친구 있어요? *Namjachingu isseoyo?*
I have a blind date tomorrow.	내일 소개팅이 있어요. *Naeil sogaetingi isseoyo.*
I broke up with my girlfriend yesterday.	어제 여자친구와 헤어졌어요. *Eoje yeojachinguwa heeojeosseoyo.*

Campus couples

Koreans have developed a specific phrase for referring to couples that meet each other while studying at university: campus couples. A "캠퍼스 커플" *kaempeoseu keopeul* is also referred to as a "CC." If you attend university in Korea, you'll be sure to hear this phrase often.

Getting to know each other

In Korea, the early stage of a relationship is called "썸" *sseom*. This word is used when you are not quite dating someone yet, but you two obviously like each other and spend a lot of time together.

Blind dates

There are two different types of blind dates in Korea: "미팅" *miting* and "소개팅" *sogaeting*. But what exactly is the difference? A 소개팅 is a one-on-one blind date organized by one of your friends. A 미팅, on the other hand, is a group blind date to which an equal number of guys and girls are invited. After talking for a while, the guys and girls all pick someone that they like and spend the rest of the evening with that person.

Meetup app

If you would like to make friends in Korea, we recommend downloading the Meetup app. Through this international app, groups of people with the same interests organize meetups to do activities together and get to know each other. Various organizations also offer inexpensive group trips for foreigners to important historical sites and interesting culture events. If you want to get to deepen your knowledge about Korea, we recommend traveling and putting yourself out there.

Chapter 7

Shopping

If you like shopping, Seoul is the perfect place for you! Myeongdong (명동) is a popular area to shop for clothes, CDs, make-up, and skincare. Korea is the mecca of make-up and skincare, so you can stock up on those sheet masks and buy presents for friends and family back home!

Namdaemun Sijang (남대문 시장), Korea's largest traditional market, is also a popular shopping destination. At Namdaemun Market, you can buy a lot of different traditional and modern items for a very good price. The number one place to find traditional Korean souvenirs is Insa-dong (인사동). There are a lot of traditional teahouses and Korean restaurants where you can rest after shopping. It is a perfect place to go on a traditional-themed shopping trip!

Korea also has many shopping malls, warehouses, and huge underground shopping centers. Although the shopping malls tend to be on the expensive side, the underground shopping centers are really cheap. No matter your budget, Korea really is the place to shop till you drop!

Stores

shop, store | 가게 *gage*, 매장 *maejang*
department store | 백화점 *baekhwajeom*
market | 시장 *sijang*
mart | 마트 *mateu*
discount store | 할인점 *harinjeom*
specialty store | 전문점 *jeonmunjeom*
shop employee | 점원 *jeomwon*
customer | 고객 *gogaek*

Useful Expressions

I am going to the market.	시장에 가고 있어요. *Sijange gago isseoyo.*
You can find it at the department store.	그건 백화점에 가면 있어요. *Geugeon baekhwajeome gamyeon isseoyo.*
I bought it at the discount store.	이건 할인점에서 샀어요. *Igeon harinjeomeseo sasseoyo.*

Attentive salespeople

Employees in Korea, especially in make-up stores, might behave differently than you are used to in your own country. They have the tendency to follow you through the whole shop. Even when you don't ask for it, they often give you advice on the products you are looking at. If you are looking to buy a sheet mask, the staff might intervene and suggest something completely different to fix your skin condition. Moreover, in popular shopping areas, employees often stand in front of the shop promoting the shop's items or sale deals. They even give you shopping baskets already stocked with a free sample to lure you into their shop. Once inside, the general rule is: the more money you spend, the more samples you get!

Transactions

to pay | (돈을) 내다 *(doneul) naeda*, 계산하다 *gyesanhada*, 지불하다 *jibulhada*, 결제하다 *gyeoljehada*

to buy | 사다 *sada*, 구매하다 *gumaehada*

to shop | 쇼핑하다 *syopinghada*

to sell | 팔다 *palda*, 판매하다 *panmaehada*

to refund | 환불하다 *hwanbulhada*

to exchange | 교환하다 *gyohwanhada*

to return | 반품하다 *banpumhada*

change | 거스름돈 *geoseureumdon*

cash | 현금 *hyeongeum*

credit card | 신용카드 *sinyongkadeu*

debit card | 체크카드 *chekeukadeu*

to withdraw money | 인출하다 *inchulhada*

ATM | 현금 인출기 *hyeongeum inchulgi*

Useful Expressions

Can I pay by credit card?	신용카드로 내도 돼요? *Sinyongkadeuro naedo dwaeyo?*
I'll pay by cash.	현금으로 낼게요. *Hyeongeumeuro naelgeyo.*
Would you please put it in a plastic bag?	봉지에 넣어주실 수 있어요? *Bongjie neoeojusil su isseoyo?*
Can I get a refund?	환불할 수 있어요? *Hwanbulhal su isseoyo?*

Shopping and paying

Most stores in Korea only accept credit cards and cash, so it can be hard to pay with a foreign debit card. Markets and smaller stores usually don't accept credit cards, or they charge a little bit more if you pay by card. Be prepared and bring some cash.

Withdrawing money

To withdraw money from a foreign bank account, look for a "global" sign at the ATM. Be aware that the bank charges a small fee. A lot of places outside of Seoul don't have global ATMs, so make sure to check that beforehand and bring enough cash. Some global ATMs don't accept all types of foreign cards. To avoid these kinds of problems, it might be useful to open a Korean bank account.

You might hear the following sentences at the counter:

Are you paying with cash?	현금으로 계산하시겠어요? *Hyeongeumeuro gyesanhasigesseoyo?*
You can get a refund or make an exchange within three days.	환불이나 교환은 3일 이내에 가능합니다. *Hwanburina gyohwaneun samil inaee ganeunghamnida.*
Thank you. Please visit us again.	감사합니다. 또 방문해 주세요. *Gamsahamnida. Tto bangmunhae juseyo.*

Prices and Sales

price | 값 *gap*, 가격 *gagyeok*

cheap | 싸다 *ssada*, 저렴하다 *jeoryeomhada*

expensive | 비싸다 *bissada*

discount | 할인 *harin*

sale | 세일 *seil*

event | 이벤트 *ibenteu*, 행사 *haengsa*

sold out | 매진 *maejin*, 품절 *pumjeol*

gift certificate, voucher | 상품권 *sangpumgwon*

product quality | 품질 *pumjil*

membership card | 회원카드 *hoewonkadeu*

Useful Expressions

How much is this?	이건 얼마예요? *Igeon eolmayeyo?*
This is too expensive!	너무 비싸요! *Neomu bissayo!*
These shoes are sold out.	이 구두는 품절됐어요. *I gududeun pumjeoldwaesseoyo.*
I want to become a member.	회원으로 가입하고 싶어요. *Hoewoneuro gaipago sipeoyo.*
Can I get a student discount?	학생 할인 받을 수 있어요? *Haksaeng harin badeul su isseoyo?*
I am just looking around.	그냥 둘러보고 있어요. *Geunyang dulleobogo isseoyo.*

Discounts and memberships

A lot of stores in Korea require you to have a membership card in order to get a discount during sales.

You may be asked:

Are you a member?	회원이세요? *Hoewoniseyo?*
Do you have a membership card?	회원카드 있으세요? *Hoewonkadeu isseuseyo?*

> **TIP**
>
> Especially when you are staying for a longer period of time and you often buy merchandise in a certain shop, it is useful to become a member. However, be aware that you often need your certificate of alien registration in order to become a member. Cafés and bakeries often have a point system that allows you to earn a free drink. Be sure to check that out if you often visit a place! On top of that, students can get a student discount at various places like movie theaters and museums. These kinds of discounts can save you a lot of money, so make sure you get those points!

Clothes and Merchandise

CLOTHES

clothes | 옷 *ot*

size | 사이즈 *saijeu*

shirt | 셔츠 *syeocheu*

T-shirt | 티셔츠 *tisyeocheu*

dress shirt | 와이셔츠 *waisyeocheu*

sweater | 스웨터 *seuweteo*

dress | 원피스 *wonpiseu*, 드레스 *deureseu*

skirt | 치마 *chima*

pants | 바지 *baji*

shorts | 반바지 *banbaji*

jeans | 청바지 *cheongbaji*

coat | 코트 *koteu*

jacket | 재킷 *jaekit*

necktie | 넥타이 *nektai*

pajamas | 잠옷 *jamot*

underwear | 속옷 *sogot*

shoes | 신발 *sinbal*

dress shoes | 구두 *gudu*

sneakers | 운동화 *undonghwa*

socks | 양말 *yangmal*

suit | 양복 *yangbok*

traditional Korean costume | 한복 *hanbok*

Useful Expressions

Is it okay to try on this skirt?	이 치마 입어 봐도 돼요? *I chima ibeo bwado dwaeyo?*
This size doesn't fit me.	사이즈가 안 맞아요. *Saijeuga an majayo.*
Do you have another size?	다른 사이즈 있어요? *Dareun saijeu isseoyo?*
Can you fix the length of these pants?	바지 길이 수선해 주실 수 있어요? *Baji giri suseonhae jusil su isseoyo?*

| Do you have a shirt to go with these pants? | 이 바지에 어울리는 셔츠가 있을까요? *I bajie eoullineun syeocheuga isseulkkayo?* |

MERCHANDISE

merchandise | 상품 *sangpum*

object, thing | 물건 *mulgeon*

cosmetics | 화장품 *hwajangpum*

souvenir | 기념품 *ginyeompum*

wallet | 지갑 *jigap*

repair | 수리 *suri*

electronics | 전자제품 *jeonjajepum*

camera | 카메라 *kamera*

computer | 컴퓨터 *keompyuteo*

cellphone | 휴대폰 *hyudaepon*

charger | 충전기 *chungjeongi*

battery | 배터리 *baeteori*

Useful Expressions

Do you sell cameras?	카메라 팔아요? *Kamera parayo?*
Where can I buy a cellphone?	휴대폰은 어디서 살 수 있어요? *Hyudaeponeun eodiseo sal su isseoyo?*
What are the specifications of this computer?	이 컴퓨터는 사양이 어떻게 되나요? *I keompyuteoneun sayangi eotteoke doenayo?*

How long does the warranty last?	품질 보증 기간은 언제까지예요? *Pumjil bojeung giganeun eonjekkajiyeyo?*
What can I take as a souvenir?	기념품으로 살 만한 것이 있을까요? *Ginyeompumeuro sal manhan geosi isseulkkayo?*

If something is broken, such as your cellphone or camera, you can ask:

Can you fix my cellphone?	휴대폰 수리해 주실 수 있어요? *Hyudaepon surihae jusil su isseoyo?*
Where can I fix my camera?	카메라 수리는 어디서 해요? *Kamera surineun eodiseo haeyo?*

University jackets

One must-buy item in Korea is your university's jacket. Korean universities generally tend to offer various goods carrying their logo and name. The baseball-style jackets are especially popular. You can see a lot of students wearing these jackets around campus areas in downtown Seoul. They tend to be popular among exchange students as well, since they are warm and comfy, plus a nice reminder of your time attending a university in Korea. Exchange students can often buy them cheaper through deals offered by student clubs. You might even be able to choose a design and put your initials on it, so check out the possibilities at your university!

Accessories

accessories | 액세서리 *aekseseori*

jewelry | 보석 *boseok*

ring | 반지 *banji*

earring | 귀걸이 *gwigeori*

necklace | 목걸이 *mokgeori*

watch | 시계 *sigye*

gloves | 장갑 *janggap*

belt | 벨트 *belteu*

hat, cap | 모자 *moja*

contact lenses | 콘택트렌즈 *kontaekteu renjeu*

glasses | 안경 *angyeong*

purse | 핸드백 *haendeubaek*

backpack | 배낭 *baenang*

Useful Expressions

Your tie goes nicely with that suit.	넥타이가 양복과 잘 어울리네요. *Nektaiga yangbokgwa jal eoullineyo.*
Your tie is crooked.	넥타이가 삐뚤어졌어요. *Nektaiga ppittureojeosseoyo.*
This belt is too tight.	벨트가 너무 조이네요. *Belteuga neomu joineyo.*
Do you wear glasses?	안경 쓰세요? *Angyeong sseuseyo?*

GETTING DRESSED

There are various Korean verbs with the meaning to wear or to put on something, but each verb can only be used in combination with certain kinds of clothing.

입다 *ipda*	to put on, wear	for basic clothes: (T-)shirt, sweater, pants, shorts, jeans, coat, jacket, pajamas, underwear, dress, skirt, suit
신다 *sinda*	to put on, wear	for footwear: shoes, sneakers, socks
쓰다 *sseuda*	to put on, wear	for headwear: glasses, hat
끼다 *kkida*	to put on	for handwear: ring, gloves
매다 *maeda*	to tie/lace (up)	for things you tie: necktie
메다 *meda*	to carry, sling	for things you wear over your shoulder: backpack, purse
차다 *chada*	to put on, wear	for things you tie around limbs: watch, bracelet
하다 *hada*	to do	for earrings, necklace

Clothing sizes and fitting room

In Korea, it can be challenging to find the right clothing size for your body type outside of global brand stores such as H&M

and Forever 21. A lot of stores only offer clothing in "free size," or one-size-fits-all, and do not allow trying on tops because wearer's make-up can leave stains on the clothes. There are even fitting rooms that don't have a top part to prevent customers from trying on T-shirts or sweaters. The clothing prices are relatively low, but you can never be quite sure if it is a hit or miss.

Beauty standards and skincare

Korean beauty trends and standards differ quite a bit from Western beauty standards. Having good skin is very important in Korea, so Koreans use a lot of skincare. Some Korean men also use basic skincare products and sometimes even basic make-up! However, Koreans don't like to have tanned skin, so a lot of skincare and make-up products contain whitening or brightening functions, which can make your face a lot whiter. Also, many products tend to make your face shiny. If you don't like this, be careful when buying skincare products and make-up.

Chapter 8

In Case of Emergency

The common emergency telephone numbers in Korea are 112 and 119. The number for fires and ambulances is 119, and 112 is for police and criminal affairs. In case you need English-speaking medical information, you can call 1339 for free information. This service line is specifically aimed for foreigners living in Seoul, but they will help you if you are in other areas as well.

Police

police | 경찰 *gyeongchal*

police station | 경찰서 *gyeongchalseo*

police car | 경찰차 *gyeongchalcha*

surveillance camera | 감시 카메라 *gamsi kamera*

accident | 사고 *sago*

thief | 도둑 *doduk*

theft | 절도 *jeoldo*

to steal | 훔치다 *humchida*

to report | 신고하다 *singohada*

victim | 피해자 *pihaeja*

witness | 목격자 *mokgyeokja*, 증인 *jeungin*

criminal | 범죄자 *beomjoeja*, 범인 *beomin*

Useful Expressions

There has been an accident over there.	저기에 사고가 났어요. *Jeogie sagoga nasseoyo.*
A thief stole my wallet and passport.	도둑이 제 지갑과 여권을 훔쳤어요. *Dodugi je jigapgwa yeogwoneul humcheosseoyo.*
Please call the police.	경찰을 불러 주세요. *Gyeongchareul bulleo juseyo.*
The police car is on its way.	경찰차가 오고 있어요. *Gyeongchalchaga ogo isseoyo.*

Please help me!	도와주세요! *Dowajuseyo!*

In Korea, you may encounter the following warning signs:

Do not enter	출입 금지 *churip geumji*
Danger	위험 *wiheom*
Warning	경고 *gyeonggo*
Non-smoking area	금연구역 *geumyeon guyeok*
No swimming	수영 금지 *suyeong geumji*
Child safety zone	어린이보호구역 *eorini bohoguyeok*

Fire Department

firefighter | 소방관 *sobanggwan*

fire station | 소방서 *sobangseo*

fire truck | 소방차 *sobangcha*

ambulance | 구급차 *gugeupcha*

fire extinguisher | 소화기 *sohwagi*

to put out (a fire) | 진화하다 *jinhwahada*

fire | 불 *bul*

blaze | 화재 *hwajae*

fire alarm | 화재 경보기 *hwajae gyeongbogi*

first aid | 응급처치 *eunggeup cheochi*

emergency exit | 비상구 *bisanggu*

emergency stairs | 비상계단 *bisanggyedan*

💬 Useful Expressions

There is a fire!	불이 났어요! *Buri nasseoyo!*
The fire alarm is ringing!	화재 경보기가 울리고 있어요! *Hwajae gyeongbogiga ulligo isseoyo!*
Where is the emergency exit?	비상구가 어디예요? *Bisangguga eodiyeyo?*
Please call 119!	119에 전화해 주세요! *ililgue jeonhwahae juseyo!*
Please call an ambulance!	구급차를 불러주세요! *Gugeupchareul bulleojuseyo!*
Where is the nearest fire station?	가장 가까운 소방서가 어디예요? *Gajang gakkaun sobangseoga eodiyeyo?*

Hospitals

hospital | 병원 *byeongwon*

doctor | 의사 *uisa*

patient | 환자 *hwanja*

nurse | 간호사 *ganhosa*

emergency room | 응급실 *eunggeupsil*

pharmacy | 약국 *yakguk*

medical insurance | 의료보험 *uiryoboheom*

hospital bills | 병원비 *byeongwonbi*

to be hospitalized | 입원하다 *ibwonhada*

to be discharged from the hospital | 퇴원하다 *toewonhada*

🗨 Useful Expressions

Does my insurance cover hospitalization bills?	입원비도 의료보험 적용이 되나요? *Ibwonbido uiryoboheom jeogyongi doenayo?*
I would like to see a doctor.	진찰받고 싶어요. *Jinchalbatgo sipeoyo.*
I was hospitalized for one week.	일주일 동안 입원했어요. *Iljuil dongan ibwonhaesseoyo.*
When can I get out of the hospital?	저는 언제 퇴원할 수 있을까요? *Jeoneun eonje toewonhal su isseulkkayo?*

Hospitals

When you are sick in Korea or need to see a doctor, go straight to the hospital. Make sure to get insurance either from your home country or Korea, depending on your length of stay and university requirements. There are special international hospitals and clinics. These charge a higher fee, but the doctors that work there speak English. The assisting staff, however, usually only speak Korean. In other hospitals, there is often an English-speaking staff member, or you can ask for an English translator. Therefore, first checking out your nearest hospital might be helpful.

    Sometimes university dormitories require you to get a health check-up at a hospital, but be careful! Some universities only accept health forms from their own university hospital or other high-ranked hospitals.

PAIN AND SYMPTOMS

symptoms | 증상 *jeungsang*

pain | 통증 *tongjeung*

wound | 상처 *sangcheo*

injury | 부상 *busang*

burn | 화상 *hwasang*

headache | 두통 *dutong*

diarrhea | 설사 *seolsa*

bruise | 멍 *meong*

toothache | 치통 *chitong*

cough | 기침 *gichim*

infection | 감염 *gamyeom*

constipation | 변비 *byeonbi*

dehydration | 탈수 *talsu*

diabetes | 당뇨 *dangnyo*

stomachache | 복통 *boktong*

to be dizzy | 어지럽다 *eojireopda*

to faint | 쓰러지다 *sseureojida*

to break | 부러지다 *bureojida*

to vomit | 토하다 *tohada*

to be bitten by mosquitoes | 모기에 물리다 *mogie mullida*

to disinfect | 소독하다 *sodokada*

itchy | 가렵다 *garyeopda*

sick | 아프다 *apeuda*

to bleed | 피를 흘리다 *pireul heullida*

to have a fever | 열이 나다 *yeori nada*

to catch a cold | 감기에 걸리다 *gamgie geollida*

Useful Expressions

I caught a cold.	감기에 걸렸어요. *Gamgie geollyeosseoyo.*
I don't feel well.	몸 상태가 안 좋아요. *Mom sangtaega an joayo.*
My arm is broken.	팔이 부러졌어요. *Pari bureojeosseoyo.*
My hand is bleeding.	손에서 피가 나요. *Soneseo piga nayo.*
Will I need surgery?	저 수술해야 하나요? *Jeo susulhaeya hanayo?*

MEDICINE AND TREATMENT

medicine | 약 *yak*

first-aid kit | 구급상자 *gugeupsangja*

prescription | 처방전 *cheobangjeon*

bandage | 붕대 *bungdae*

birth control pill | 피임약 *piimnyak*

side effect | 부작용 *bujagyong*

treatment | 치료 *chiryo*

antibiotic | 항생제 *hangsaengje*

vaccination | 예방접종 *yebangjeopjong*

ointment | 연고 *yeongo*

surgery | 수술 *susul*

painkiller | 진통제 *jintongje*

Useful Expressions

Do you have painkillers?	진통제 있으세요? *Jintongje isseuseyo?*
I am on medication for diabetes.	당뇨약을 먹고 있어요. *Dangnyoyageul meokgo isseoyo.*
This medicine is effective against a headache.	이 약은 두통에 좋아요. *I yageun dutonge joayo.*
I need to disinfect the wound.	상처를 소독해야 돼요. *Sangcheoreul sodokaeya dwaeyo.*

THE BODY

body | 몸 *mom*

head | 머리 *meori*

face | 얼굴 *eolgul*

eye | 눈 *nun*

mouth | 입 *ip*

lip | 입술 *ipsul*

nose | 코 *ko*

ear | 귀 *gwi*

throat | 목 *mok*

teeth | 이 *i*

shoulder | 어깨 *eokkae*

arm | 팔 *pal*

wrist | 팔목 *palmok*

waist | 허리 *heori*

hand | 손 *son*

finger | 손가락 *songarak*

back | 등 *deung*

chest | 가슴 *gaseum*

stomach | 배 *bae*

butt | 엉덩이 *eongdeongi*

leg | 다리 *dari*

knee | 무릎 *mureup*

foot | 발 *bal*

ankle | 발목 *balmok*

skin | 피부 *pibu*

muscle | 근육 *geunyuk*

bone | 뼈 *ppyeo*

heart | 심장 *simjang*

liver | 간 *gan*

lung | 폐 *pye*

stomach | 위 *wi*

appendix | 맹장 *maengjang*

brain | 뇌 *noe*

intestine | 장 *jang*

💬 Useful Expressions

Where does it hurt?	어디가 아프세요? *Eodiga apeuseyo?*
My waist hurts.	허리가 아파요. *Heoriga apayo.*

Plastic surgery

Want to be prettier? Then Korea, specifically Gangnam in Seoul, is the place to be. The country spends a lot on medical development and promotes medical tourism. Korea is especially known for its clinics that provide high quality yet affordable plastic surgery, 성형 수술 *seonghyeong susul*. You can find plastic surgery commercials everywhere, from the subway to newspapers. This is because the beauty standards are high in Korea, and many Koreans, especially women, feel the pressure to live up to these standards every day. Because of this, Koreans undergo plastic surgery more often than in other countries. A common graduation gift for young female high school graduates is double-eyelid surgery.

Word List

A

above, top / 위 *wi*
absolute grading / 절대평가 *jeoldae pyeongga*
accessories / 액세서리 *aekseseori*
accident / 사고 *sago*
addition / 추가 *chuga*
a few days / 며칠 *myeochil*
afternoon / 오후 *ohu*
air conditioner / 에어컨 *eeokeon*
air conditioning / 냉방 *naengbang*
airplane / 비행기 *bihaenggi*
airport / 공항 *gonghang*
alien registration card / 외국인 등록증 *oegugin deungnokjeung*
a little, a bit / 조금 *jogeum*
all day long / 하루 종일 *haru jongil*
alone / 혼자 *honja*
a long time / 오랫동안 *oraetdongan*
a lot / 많이 *mani*
always / 항상 *hangsang*
a.m. / 오전 *ojeon*
ambulance / 구급차 *gugeupcha*
amusement park / 놀이공원 *norigongwon*

ankle / 발목 *balmok*
antibiotic / 항생제 *hangsaengje*
apartment / 아파트 *apateu*
appendix / 맹장 *maengjang*
apple / 사과 *sagwa*
April / 4월 *sawol*
apron / 앞치마 *apchima*
Arabic / 아랍어 *arabeo*
architecture / 건축학 *geonchukhak*
area, region / 지역 *jiyeok*
arm / 팔 *pal*
(to) arrive / 도착하다 *dochakhada*
assignment / 과제 *gwaje*
ATM / 현금 인출기 *hyeongeum inchulgi*
August / 8월 *parwol*
aunt / 이모 *imo*
Australia / 호주 *hoju*
autumn / 가을 *gaeul*
Awesome! (Jackpot!) / 대박 *daebak*

B

bachelor's degree / 학사 *haksa*
back / 등 *deung*

backpack / 배낭 *baenang*

backpacking / 배낭여행 *baenangyeohaeng*

bad / 나쁘다 *nappeuda*

badminton / 배드민턴 *baedeuminteon*

baggage / 짐 *jim*

ball / 공 *gong*

banana / 바나나 *banana*

bandage / 붕대 *bungdae*

bank / 은행 *eunhang*

bar / 술집 *suljip*

baseball / 야구 *yagu*

basketball / 농구 *nonggu*

bathroom / 화장실 *hwajangsil*

bathtub / 욕조 *yokjo*

battery / 배터리 *baeteori*

beach / 해변 *haebyeon*

bean paste stew / 된장찌개 *doenjang jjigae*

bed / 침대 *chimdae*

bedroom / 침실 *chimsil*

beef / 소고기 *sogogi*

beer / 맥주 *maekju*

beer mixed with soju / 소맥 *somaek*

behind, back / 뒤 *dwi*

below, bottom / 밑 *mit*, 아래 *arae*

belt / 벨트 *belteu*

beside, side / 옆 *yeop*

beverage / 음료(수) *eumnyo(su)*

bibimbap (rice mixed with vegetables and beef) / 비빔밥 *bibimbap*

bicycle / 자전거 *jajeongeo*

big / 크다 *keuda*

biology / 생물학 *saengmulhak*

birth control pill / 피임약 *piimnyak*

(to be) bitten by mosquitoes / 모기에 물리다 *mogie mullida*

bitter / 쓰다 *sseuda*

black / 검은색 *geomeunsaek*

bland / 싱겁다 *singgeopda*

blanket / 이불 *ibul*

blaze / 화재 *hwajae*

(to) bleed / 피를 흘리다 *pireul heullida*

blind date / 소개팅 *sogaeting*

blue / 파란색 *paransaek*

boarding house / 하숙집 *hasukjip*

body / 몸 *mom*

boiler / 보일러 *boilleo*

bone / 뼈 *ppyeo*

book / 책 *chaek*

bookshelf / 책장 *chaekjang*

bookstore / 서점 *seojeom*

boring / 지루하다 *jiruhada*

(to) borrow / 빌리다 *billida*

bottle / 병 *byeong*

bowl / 그릇 *geureut*

bowl of rice / 공기밥 *gonggibap*

boyfriend / 남자친구 (남친) *namjachingu (namchin)*

brain / 뇌 *noe*

braised spicy chicken with vegetables / 찜닭 *jjimdak*

bread / 빵 *ppang*

(to) break / 부러지다 *bureojida*

breakfast / 아침 *achim*

(to) break up / 헤어지다 *heeojida*

bridge / 다리 *dari*

brown / 갈색 *galsaek*

bruise / 멍 *meong*

Buddhist temple / 사찰 *sachal*, 절 *jeol*

bulgogi (grilled marinated beef) / 불고기 *bulgogi*

burn / 화상 *hwasang*

bus / 버스 *beoseu*

bus stop / 버스 정류장 *beoseu jeongnyujang*

business administration / 경영학 *gyeongyeonghak*

busy / 바쁘다 *bappeuda*

butt / 엉덩이 *eongdeongi*

(to) buy / 사다 *sada*, 구매하다 *gumaehada*

---- C ----

café / 카페 *kape*

camera / 카메라 *kamera*

camping / 캠핑 *kaemping*

campus / 캠퍼스 *kaempeoseu*

(to) catch a cold / 감기에 걸리다 *gamgie geollida*

car / 자동차 *jadongcha*

cash / 현금 *hyeongeum*

cellphone / 휴대폰 *hyudaepon*

chair / 의자 *uija*

change / 거스름돈 *geoseureumdon*

charger / 충전기 *chungjeongi*

cheap / 싸다 *ssada*, 저렴하다 *jeoryeomhada*

cheers / 건배 *geonbae*

cheese / 치즈 *chijeu*

chemistry / 화학 *hwahak*

chest / 가슴 *gaseum*

chicken / 치킨 *chikin*

chicken and beer / 치맥 *chimaek*

child safety zone / 어린이보호구역 *eorinibohoguyeok*

China / 중국 *jungguk*

Chinese / 중국어 *junggugeo*

Chinese food / 중식 *jungsik*

(a pair of) chopsticks / 젓가락 *jeotgarak*

church / 교회 *gyohoe*

city / 도시 *dosi*

class, lesson / 수업 *sueop*

clean / 깨끗하다 *kkaekkeutada*

- close (to/by) / 가깝다 *gakkapda*
- clothes / 옷 *ot*
- cloudy / 구름이 잔뜩 끼다 *gureumi jantteuk kkida*
- club / 클럽 *keulleop*
- coat / 코트 *koteu*
- cocktail / 칵테일 *kakteil*
- (iced) coffee / (아이스) 커피 *(aiseu) keopi*
- cold / 춥다 *chupda*, 차갑다 *chagapda*
- college sweethearts / 캠퍼스 커플 (CC) *kaempeoseu keopeul*
- (to) come / 오다 *oda*
- computer / 컴퓨터 *keompyuteo*
- concert / 콘서트 *konseoteu*
- constipation / 변비 *byeonbi*
- contact lenses / 콘택트렌즈 *kontaekteu renjeu*
- contract / 계약서 *gyeyakseo*
- convenience store / 편의점 *pyeonuijeom*
- (to) cook / 요리하다 *yorihada*
- cooking, dishes / 요리 *yori*
- cool / 멋있다 *meositda*
- (to) copy / 복사하다 *boksahada*
- copy room / 복사실 *boksasil*
- cosmetics / 화장품 *hwajangpum*
- cough / 기침 *gichim*
- country / 국가 *gukga*, 나라 *nara*
- course registration / 수강신청 *sugang sincheong*
- cramming / 벼락치기 *byeorakchigi*
- credit card / 신용카드 *sinyongkadeu*
- criminal / 범죄자 *beomjoeja*, 범인 *beomin*
- crosswalk / 횡단보도 *hoengdanbodo*
- culture / 문화 *munhwa*
- cup / 컵 *keop*
- curfew / 통행금지 (통금) *tonghaeng geumji (tonggeum)*
- customer / 고객 *gogaek*
- cute / 귀엽다 *gwiyeopda*

D

- (to) dance / 춤추다 *chumchuda*
- danger / 위험 *wiheom*
- (to) date / 데이트하다 *deiteuhada*
- date / 데이트 *deiteu*
- day / 일 *il*
- daytime / 낮 *nat*
- deadline / 마감 *magam*
- debit card / 체크카드 *chekeukadeu*
- December / 12월 *sibiwol*
- dehydration / 탈수 *talsu*
- delicious / 맛있다 *masittta*
- delivery / 배달 *baedal*
- (to) depart / 출발하다 *chulbalhada*
- department store / 백화점

baekhwajeom

deposit / 보증금 *bojeunggeum*

desk / 책상 *chaeksang*

detergent, cleaner / 세제 *seje*

diabetes / 당뇨 *dangnyo*

diarrhea / 설사 *seolsa*

dictionary / 사전 *sajeon*

different / 다르다 *dareuda*

difficult / 어렵다 *eoryeopda*

dinner / 저녁 *jeonyeok*

dirty / 더럽다 *deoreopda*

(to be) discharged from the hospital / 퇴원하다 *toewonhada*

discount / 할인 *harin*

discount store / 할인점 *harinjeom*

(to) disinfect / 소독하다 *sodokada*

(to be) dizzy / 어지럽다 *eojireopda*

(to) do grocery shopping / 장보다 *jangboda*

do not enter / 출입 금지 *churip geumji*

doctor / 의사 *uisa*

doctorate / 박사 *baksa*

door / 문 *mun*

dormitory / 기숙사 *gisuksa*

dress / 드레스 *deureseu*

dress shirt / 와이셔츠 *waisyeocheu*

dress shoes / 구두 *gudu*

(to) drink / 마시다 *masida*

(to) drive / 운전하다 *unjeonhada*

driver / 운전기사 *unjeongisa*

driver's license / 운전면허 *unjeonmyeonheo*

dry / 마르다 *mareuda*

during / 동안 *dongan*

E

ear / 귀 *gwi*

early / 이르다 *ireuda*

early / 일찍 *iljjik*

earring / 귀걸이 *gwigeori*

easy / 쉽다 *swipda*

(to) eat / 먹다 *meokda*

eating alone / 혼밥 *honbap*

eating out / 외식 *oesik*

economics / 경제학 *gyeongjehak*

education / 교육학 *gyoyukhak*

egg / 계란 *gyeran*

electrical engineering / 전기공학 *jeongigonghak*

electricity / 전기 *jeongi*

electronics / 전자제품 *jeonjajepum*

elevator / 엘리베이터 *ellibeiteo*

emergency exit / 비상구 *bisanggu*

emergency room / 응급실 *eunggeupsil*

emergency stairs / 비상계단 *bisanggyedan*

England / 영국 *yeongguk*

English / 영어 *yeongeo*

entrance / 입구 *ipgu*

entrance ticket / 입장권 *ipjanggwon*

essay / 에세이 *esei*

evening / 저녁 *jeonyeok*

event / 이벤트 *ibenteu*, 행사 *haengsa*

every day / 매일 *maeil*

every week / 매주 *maeju*

exam / 시험 *siheom*

(to) exchange / 교환하다 *gyohwanhada*

exchange student / 교환학생 *gyohwan haksaeng*

excuse me (when asking for attention) / 저기요 *jeogiyo*

(to) exercise / 운동하다 *undonghada*

exit / 출구 *chulgu*

expensive / 비싸다 *bissada*

eye / 눈 *nun*

F

face / 얼굴 *eolgul*

fail / 불합격 *bulhapgyeok*

(to) faint / 쓰러지다 *sseureojida*

far (from) / 멀다 *meolda*

father / 아버지 *abeoji*, 아빠 *appa*

February / 2월 *iwol*

fee / 요금 *yogeum*

festival / 축제 *chukje*

few / 적다 *jeokda*

final examination / 기말고사 *gimalgosa*

finger / 손가락 *songarak*

fire / 불 *bul*

fire alarm / 화재 경보기 *hwajae gyeongbogi*

fire extinguisher / 소화기 *sohwagi*

Fire Friday / 불금 *bulgeum*

fire station / 소방서 *sobangseo*

fire truck / 소방차 *sobangcha*

firefighter / 소방관 *sobanggwan*

first / 첫 번째 *cheot beonjjae*

first-aid kit / 구급상자 *gugeupsangja*

first aid / 응급처치 *eunggeup cheochi*

fish / 생선 *saengseon*

foot / 발 *bal*

foreign language / 외국어 *oegugeo*

foreign student / 유학생 *yuhaksaeng*

fork / 포크 *pokeu*

France / 프랑스 *peurangseu*

free / 무료 *muryo*

French / 프랑스어 *peurangseueo*

Friday / 금요일 *geumyoil*

fried food / 튀김 *twigim*

fried rice / 볶음밥 *bokkeumbap*

front, in front of / 앞 *ap*

fruit / 과일 *gwail*

(to be) full / 배부르다 *baebureuda*

fun / 재미있다 *jaemiitda*

G

game / 게임 *geim*, 경기 *gyeonggi*

garlic / 마늘 *maneul*

gas / 가스 *gaseu*

(to) get drunk / 취하다 *chwihada*

(to) get off, out of (a vehicle) / 내리다 *naerida*

(to) get on, into (a vehicle) / 타다 *tada*

German / 독일어 *dogireo*

Germany / 독일 *dogil*

gift certificate, voucher / 상품권 *sangpumgwon*

gimbap (dried seaweed rolls) / 김밥 *gimbap*

girlfriend / 여자친구 (여친) *yeojachingu (yeochin)*

(to) give / 주다 *juda*

glass / 잔 *jan*

glasses / 안경 *angyeong*

gloves / 장갑 *janggap*

(to) go / 가다 *gada*

(to) go out / 사귀다 *sagwida*

going Dutch / 더치페이 *deochipei*

gold / 금색 *geumsaek*

good / 좋다 *jota*

goodbye (when someone is leaving) / 안녕히 가세요 *annyeonghi gaseyo*

goodbye (when someone is staying) / 안녕히 계세요 *annyeonghi gyeseyo*

good place to eat / 맛집 *matjip*

gosiwon / 고시원 *gosiwon*

grade, year of study / 학년 *hangnyeon*

grade / 성적 *seongjeok*

graduate school / 대학원 *daehagwon*

gray / 회색 *hoesaek*

greasy / 느끼하다 *neukkihada*

green / 녹색 *noksaek*

green-onion pancake / 파전 *pajeon*

grill / 불판 *bulpan*

group blind date / 미팅 *miting*

guitar / 기타 *gita*

guy friend / 남자 사람 친구 (남사친) *namja saram chingu (namsachin)*

gym / 헬스장 *helseujang*

H

ham / 햄 *haem*

hand / 손 *son*

handsome / 잘생기다 *jalsaenggida*

hat, cap / 모자 *moja*

(to) hate / 싫어하다 *sireohada*

(to) have a casual dating relationship / 썸타다 *sseomtada*

(to) have a drink / 한 잔 하다 *han jan hada*

(to) have a fever / 열이 나다 *yeori nada*

(to) have a party / 파티를 하다 *patireul hada*

hazy / 흐리다 *heurida*

head / 머리 *meori*

headache / 두통 *dutong*

heart / 심장 *simjang*

heating / 난방 *nanbang*

hello / 안녕하세요 *annyeonghaseyo*

here / 여기 *yeogi*

high / 높다 *nopda*

highway / 고속도로 *gosokdoro*

(to) hike / 등산하다 *deungsanhada*

history / 역사학 *yeoksahak*

hospital / 병원 *byeongwon*

hospital bills / 병원비 *byeongwonbi*

(to be) hospitalized / 입원하다 *ibwonhada*

hot / 덥다 *deopda*, 뜨겁다 *tteugeopda*

hour / 시간 *sigan*

house / 집 *jip*

how / 어떻게 *eotteoke*

how many / 몇 *myeot*

how much / 얼마 *eolma*

(to be) hungry / 배고프다 *baegopeuda*

I

I'm sorry (casual) / 미안합니다 *mianhamnida*

I'm sorry (formal) / 죄송합니다 *joesonghamnida*

ice cream / 아이스크림 *aiseukeurim*

individual / 개인 *gaein*

infection / 감염 *gamyeom*

ingredients / 재료 *jaeryo*

injury / 부상 *busang*

inside / 안 *an*

instant noodles / 라면 *ramyeon*

(wireless) internet / (무선) 인터넷 *(museon) inteonet*

internet café / PC방 *pissibang*

intersection / 사거리 *sageori*

intestine / 장 *jang*

it's okay / 괜찮아요 *gwaenchanayo*

itchy / 가렵다 *garyeopda*

ivory / 아이보리색 *aiborisaek*

jacket / 재킷 *jaekit*

J

January / 1월 *irwol*

Japan / 일본 *ilbon*

Japanese / 일본어 *ilboneo*

Japanese food / 일식 *ilsik*
jeans / 청바지 *cheongbaji*
jewelry / 보석 *boseok*
jogging / 조깅 *joging*
joint, shared / 공용 *gongyong*
juice / 주스 *juseu*
July / 7월 *chirwol*
June / 6월 *yuwol*
junior / 후배 *hubae*
just / 그냥 *geunyang*

---------- K ----------

karaoke / 노래방 *noraebang*
kimchi / 김치 *gimchi*
kitchen / 부엌 *bueok*, 주방 *jubang*
knee / 무릎 *mureup*
knife / 칼 *kal*, 나이프 *naipeu*
Korea / 한국 *hanguk*
Korean / 한국어 *hangugeo*
Korean food / 한식 *hansik*
Korean sauna / 찜질방 *jjimjilbang*

---------- L ----------

language exchange / 언어교환 *eoneo gyohwan*
laptop / 노트북 *noteubuk*
last / 지난 *jinan*
last year / 작년 *jangnyeon*
late / 늦다 *neutda*

lately / 요즘 *yojeum*
laundry detergent / 세탁용 세제 *setakyong seje*
law / 법학 *beophak*
lecture / 강의 *gangui*
lecture room / 강의실 *ganguisil*
left / 왼쪽 *oenjjok*
leg / 다리 *dari*
(to) lend / 빌려주다 *billyeojuda*
lettuce / 상추 *sangchu*
library / 도서관 *doseogwan*
light / 불 *bul*, 등 *deung*
(to) like / 좋아하다 *joahada*
linguistics / 언어학 *eoneohak*
lip / 입술 *ipsul*
liquor / 술 *sul*
(to) listen / 듣다 *deutta*
literature / 문학 *munhak*
liver / 간 *gan*
living room / 거실 *geosil*
long time no see / 오랜만이에요 *oraenmanieyo*
low / 낮다 *natda*
lunch / 점심 *jeomsim*
lung / 폐 *pye*

---------- M ----------

major / 전공 *jeongong*
(to) make a U-turn / 유턴하다 *yuteonhada*

makgeolli / 막걸리 *makgeolli*

man / 남자 *namja*

many / 많다 *manta*

map / 지도 *jido*

March / 3월 *samwol*

market / 시장 *sijang*

mart / 마트 *mateu*

master's degree / 석사 *seoksa*

May / 5월 *owol*

meal / 식사 *siksa*

meat / 고기 *gogi*

mechanical engineering / 기계공학 *gigyegonghak*

medical insurance / 의료보험 *uiryoboheom*

medicine / 의학 *uihak*

medicine / 약 *yak*

membership card / 회원카드 *hoewonkadeu*

membership training (MT) / 엠티 *emti*

mentalshock / 멘붕 (멘탈붕괴) *menbung (mentalbunggoe)*

menu / 메뉴 *menyu*

merchandise / 상품 *sangpum*

microwave / 전자레인지 *jeonjareinji*

middle-aged man / 아저씨 *ajeossi*

middle-aged woman / 아줌마 *ajumma*, 아주머니 *ajumeoni*

midterm examination / 중간고사 *junggangosa*

mild / 순하다 *sunhada*

milk / 우유 *uyu*

mineral water / 생수 *saengsu*

minor / 부전공 *bujeongong*

minute / 분 *bun*

mirror / 거울 *geoul*

Monday / 월요일 *woryoil*

money / 돈 *don*

month / 월 *weol*

monthly rent / 월세 *wolse*

morning / 아침 *achim*

mother / 어머니 *eomeoni*, 엄마 *eomma*

mother tongue, native language / 모국어 *mogugeo*

mountain / 산 *san*

mouth / 입 *ip*

movie / 영화 *yeonghwa*

Mr. / Mrs. / Ms. / –씨 *ssi*

muscle / 근육 *geunyuk*

museum / 박물관 *bangmulgwan*

music / 음악 *eumak*

musical / 뮤지컬 *myujikeol*

musical instrument / 악기 *akgi*

N

narrow / 좁다 *jopda*

necklace / 목걸이 *mokgeori*

necktie / 넥타이 *nektai*

neighborhood, town /

동네 *dongne*

neighborhood, vicinity / 근처 *geuncheo*

newspaper / 신문 *sinmun*

next time / 다음번 *daeumbun*

next year / 내년 *naenyeon*

night / 밤 *bam*

no / 아니오 *anio*

no swimming / 수영 금지 *suyeong geumji*

noisy / 시끄럽다 *sikkeureopda*

non-smoking area / 금연구역 *geumyeon guyeok*

noodles / 국수 *guksu*

nose / 코 *ko*

not good tasting / 맛없다 *madeopda*

notes / 노트 *noteu*

November / 11월 *sibirwol*

now / 지금 *jigeum*

nurse / 간호사 *ganhosa*

O

object, thing / 물건 *mulgeon*

__ o'clock / __시 *si*

October / 10월 *siwol*

octopus / 문어 *muneo*

often / 종종 *jongjong*

oh my god / 헐 *heol*

ointment / 연고 *yeongo*

older male (for men) / 형 *hyeong*

older male (for women) / 오빠 *oppa*

older woman (for men) / 누나 *nuna*

older woman (for women) / 언니 *eonni*

on the house / 서비스 *seobiseu*

on the opposite side / 맞은편 *majeunpyeon*

one-way / 편도 *pyeondo*

one shot / 원샷 *wonsyat*

onion / 양파 *yangpa*

orange / 주황색 *juhwangsaek*

order / 주문 *jumun*

oven / 오븐 *obeun*

over there / 저기 *jeogi*

P

p.m. / 오후 *ohu*

pain / 통증 *tongjeung*

painkiller / 진통제 *jintongje*

pajamas / 잠옷 *jamot*

palace / 궁궐 *gunggwol*

pants / 바지 *baji*

parents / 부모님 *bumonim*

park / 공원 *gongwon*

parking lot / 주차장 *juchajang*

pass / 합격 *hapgyeok*

passport / 여권 *yeogwon*

(to) pay / (돈을) 내다 *(doneul) naeda*, 계산하다 *gyesanhada*, 지불하다 *jibulhada*, 결제하다 *gyeoljehada*

patient / 환자 *hwanja*

(to) play (musical instrument) / 연주하다 *yeonjuhada*

pen / 펜 *pen*

pencil / 연필 *yeonpil*

pencil case / 필통 *piltong*

person / 사람 *saram*

pharmacy / 약국 *yakguk*

phone number / 전화번호 *jeonhwabeonho*

physics / 물리학 *mullihak*

piano / 피아노 *piano*

pillow / 베개 *begae*

pink / 분홍색 *bunhongsaek*

plate / 접시 *jeopsi*

platform / 승강장 *seunggangjang*

play / 연극 *yeonguek*

police / 경찰 *gyeongchal*

police car / 경찰차 *gyeongchalcha*

police station / 경찰서 *gyeongchalseo*

political science / 정치학 *jeongchihak*

pork / 돼지고기 *dwaejigogi*

pork belly / 삼겹살 *samgyeopsal*

porridge / 죽 *juk*

portion / 인분 *inbun*

post office / 우체국 *ucheguk*

potato / 감자 *gamja*

preparation(s) / 예습 *yeseup*

prescription / 처방전 *cheobangjeon*

presentation / 발표 *balpyo*

pretty / 예쁘다 *yeppeuda*

price / 값 *gap*, 가격 *gagyeok*

(to) print (out) / 인쇄하다 *inswaehada*

private lesson / 과외 *gwaoe*

probably / 아마 *ama*

product quality / 품질 *pumjil*

professor / 교수님 *gyosunim*

professor's office / 연구실 *yeongusil*

psychology / 심리학 *simnihak*

public transportation / 대중교통 *daejung gyotong*

purple / 보라색 *borasaek*

purse / 핸드백 *haendeubaek*

(to) put out (a fire) / 진화하다 *jinhwahada*

Q

question / 질문 *jilmun*

quick / 빠르다 *ppareuda*

quickly / 빨리 *ppalli*

quiet / 조용하다 *joyonghada*

R

radio / 라디오 *radio*

raining / 비가 오다 *biga oda*

rainy season / 장마 *jangma*

(to) read / 읽다 *ikda*

reading books / 독서 *dokseo*

receipt / 영수증 *yeongsujeung*

(to) receive / 받다 *batda*

red / 빨간색 *ppalgansaek*

red pepper paste / 고추장 *gochujang*

refrigerator / 냉장고 *naengjanggo*

(to) refund / 환불하다 *hwanbulhada*

relative grading / 상대평가 *sangdae pyeongga*

rental housing / 전세 *jeonse*

repair / 수리 *suri*

(to) report / 신고하다 *singohada*

(to) reserve / 예약하다 *yeyakhada*

restaurant / 식당 *sikdang*

(to) return / 반품하다 *banpumhada*

review / 복습 *bokseup*

right / 오른쪽 *oreunjjok*

right / 맞다 *matda*

ring / 반지 *banji*

river / 강 *gang*

road (for cars) / 차도 *chado*

room rent / 방세 *bangse*

roommate / 룸메이트 *rummeiteu*

round-trip / 왕복 *wangbok*

round two / 2차 *icha*

(to) run / 뛰다 *ttwida*

rush hour / 러시아워 *reosiawo*

Russia / 러시아 *reosia*

Russian / 러시아어 *reosiaeo*

S

salad / 샐러드 *saelleodeu*

sale / 세일 *seil*

salt / 소금 *sogeum*

salty / 짜다 *jjada*

same / 같다 *gatda*

Saturday / 토요일 *toyoil*

schedule / 시간표 *siganpyo*

score / 점수 *jeomsu*

sea / 바다 *bada*

season / 계절 *gyejeol*

seaweed / 미역 *miyeok*

second / 초 *cho*

second language / 제2외국어 *jeioegugeo*

self-serve / 셀프 *selpeu*

(to) sell / 팔다 *palda*, 판매하다 *panmaehada*

semester / 학기 *hakgi*

senior / 선배 *seonbae*

separately / 각자 *gakja*

September / 9월 *guwol*

(to) set the table / 상을 차리다 *sangeul charida*

shampoo / 샴푸 *syampu*

shaved ice with syrup / 빙수 *bingsu*

shower / 샤워기 *syawogi*

shirt / 셔츠 *syeocheu*

shoes / 신발 *sinbal*

(to) shop / 쇼핑하다 *syopinghada*

shop employee / 점원 *jeomwon*

shop, store / 가게 *gage*, 매장 *maejang*

shorts / 반바지 *banbaji*

shoulder / 어깨 *eokkae*

shower room / 샤워실 *syawosil*, 욕실 *yoksil*

shrimp / 새우 *saeu*

sick / 아프다 *apeuda*

side dish / 반찬 *banchan*

side effect / 부작용 *bujagyong*

sidewalk / 인도 *indo*

(to go) sightseeing / 관광(하다) *gwangwang(hada)*

silver / 은색 *eunsaek*

(to) sing a song / 노래를 부르다 *noraereul bureuda*

sink, basin / 싱크대 *singkeudae*, 세면대 *semyeondae*

(to) sit / 앉다 *anda*

size / 사이즈 *saijeu*

(ice) skating / (아이스) 스케이트 *(aiseu) seukeiteu*

skiing / 스키 *seuki*

skin / 피부 *pibu*

skirt / 치마 *chima*

(to) sleep / 자다 *jada*

slow / 느리다 *neurida*

small / 작다 *jakda*

small octopus / 낙지 *nakji*

sneakers / 운동화 *undonghwa*

snowing / 눈이 오다 *nuni oda*

soccer / 축구 *chukgu*

socks / 양말 *yangmal*

sofa, couch / 소파 *sopa*

soft tofu stew / 순두부찌개 *sundubu jjigae*

soju / 소주 *soju*

sold out / 매진 *maejin*, 품절 *pumjeol*

soup / 국 *guk*

sour / 시다 *sida*

souvenir / 기념품 *ginyeompum*

soy sauce / 간장 *ganjang*

soybean paste / 된장 *doenjang*

spacious / 넓다 *neolda*

Spanish / 스페인어 *seupeineo*

(to) speak / 말하다 *malhada*

specialty store / 전문점 *jeonmunjeom*

spicy / 맵다 *maepda*

spoon / 숟가락 *sutgarak*

sports / 스포츠 *seupocheu*
spring / 봄 *bom*
squid / 오징어 *ojingeo*
(to) stand / 서다 *seoda*
station / 역 *yeok*
(to) steal / 훔치다 *humchida*
stir-fried rice cake / 떡볶이 *tteokbokki*
stomach / 배 *bae*, 위 *wi*
stomachache / 복통 *boktong*
stone pot / 돌솥 *dolsot*
(to) stop (car, taxi) / 세우다 *seuda*
strawberry / 딸기 *ttalgi*
street performance / 거리 공연 *geori gongyeon*
street, distance / 거리 *geori*
street, route / 길 *gil*
streetlight / 가로등 *garodeung*
(to) stroll / 산책하다 *sanchaekhada*
strong / 자극적이다 *jageukjeogida*
student cafeteria / 학생식당 *haksaeng sikdang*
student ID card / 학생증 *haksaengjeung*
student union building / 학생회관 *haksaeng hoegwan*
studio (apartment) / 원룸 *wollum*
study / 공부하다 *gongbuhada*
study (room) / 서재 *seojae*
subject / 과목 *gwamok*

(to) submit, hand in / 제출하다 *jechulhada*
subtitles / 자막 *jamak*
subway / 지하철 *jihacheol*
subway line / 호선 *hoseon*
sugar / 설탕 *seoltang*
suit / 양복 *yangbok*
summer / 여름 *yeoreum*
Sunday / 일요일 *iryoil*
sunny / 맑다 *makda*
sure, I'm in / 콜 *kol*
surgery / 수술 *susul*
surroundings / 주변 *jubyeon*
surveillance camera / 감시 카메라 *gamsi kamera*
sweater / 스웨터 *seuweteo*
sweet / 달다 *dalda*
swimming / 수영 *suyeong*
symptoms / 증상 *jeungsang*

T

T-shirt / 티셔츠 *tisyeocheu*
table tennis / 탁구 *takgu*
taekwondo / 태권도 *taegwondo*
take-out / 포장 *pojang*
take classes / 수강하다 *suganghada*
take notes / 필기하다 *pilgihada*
tangerine / 귤 *gyul*
taste / 맛 *mat*

taxi / 택시 *taeksi*

taxi stand / 택시 승차장 *taeksi seungchajang*

tea / 차 *cha*

teach / 가르치다 *gareuchida*

teacher / 선생님 *seonsaengnim*

teaching assistant / 조교 *jogyo*

teaching materials / 교재 *gyojae*

teeth / 이 *i*

television / 텔레비전 *tellebijeon*

tennis / 테니스 *teniseu*

thank you (casual) / 고맙습니다 *gomapseumnida*

thank you (formal) / 감사합니다 *gamsahamnida*

the best, extremely (when used as an adjective) / 짱 *jjang*

the day after tomorrow / 모레 *more*

the humidity is high / 습도가 높다 *seupdoga nopda*

theater / 극장 *geukjang*

theft / 절도 *jeoldo*

there / 거기 *geogi*

thesis / 논문 *nonmun*

thief / 도둑 *doduk*

(to be) thirsty / 목이 마르다 *mogi mareuda*

this time / 이번 *ibeon*

this year / 올해 *olhae*

throat / 목 *mok*

Thursday / 목요일 *mogyoil*

ticket / 티켓 *tiket*, 표 *pyo*

ticket machine / 티켓 발매기 *tiket balmaegi*

ticket office / 매표소 *maepyoso*

tired / 피곤하다 *pigonhada*

today / 오늘 *oneul*

tofu / 두부 *dubu*

together / 같이 *gachi*

toilet / 변기 *byeongi*

toilet paper / 휴지 *hyuji*

tomorrow / 내일 *naeil*

too / 너무 *neomu*

toothache / 치통 *chitong*

toothbrush / 칫솔 *chitsol*

toothpaste / 치약 *chiyak*

tourist / 관광객 *gwangwanggaek*

tourist information center / 관광 안내소 *gwangwang annaeso*

towel / 수건 *sugeon*

traditional Korean costume / 한복 *hanbok*

traffic is backed up / 길이 막히다 *giri makida*

traffic jam / 교통 체증 *gyotong chejeung*

traffic light / 신호등 *sinhodeung*

traffic sign / 표지판 *pyojipan*

train / 기차 *gicha*

transfer / 환승 *hwanseung*

(to) transfer / 갈아타다 *garatada*, 환승하다 *hwanseunghada*

transportation / 교통 *gyotong*

transportation card / 교통카드 *gyotongkadeu*

transportation cost / 교통비 *gyotongbi*

trashcan / 쓰레기통 *sseuregitong*

treatment / 치료 *chiryo*

Tuesday / 화요일 *hwayoil*

(to) turn left / 좌회전하다 *jwahoejeonhada*

(to) turn right / 우회전하다 *uhoejeonhada*

TV drama / 드라마 *deurama*

--- **U** ---

U.S.A / 미국 *miguk*

uncle / 삼촌 *samchon*

underpass / 지하도 *jihado*

underwear / 속옷 *sogot*

university / 대학교 *daehakgyo*

university club / 동아리 *dongari*

university student / 대학생 *daehaksaeng*

unlimited refill / 무한리필 *muhanripil*

usually / 보통 *botong*

--- **V** ---

vacation / 방학 *banghak*

vaccination / 예방접종 *yebangjeopjong*

variety show / 예능 *yeneung*

vegetables / 야채 *yachae*

very / 아주 *aju*

victim / 피해자 *pihaeja*

village / 마을 *maeul*

vinegar / 식초 *sikcho*

violin / 바이올린 *baiollin*

visa / 비자 *bija*

(to) vomit / 토하다 *tohada*

--- **W** ---

waist / 허리 *heori*

(to) wait / 기다리다 *gidarida*

(to) walk / 걷다 *geotda*

wallet / 지갑 *jigap*

wardrobe, closet / 옷장 *otjang*

warm / 따뜻하다 *ttatteutada*

warning / 경고 *gyeonggo*

washing machine / 세탁기 *setakgi*

watch / 시계 *sigye*

(to) watch / 보다 *boda*

water / 물 *mul*

water purifier / 정수기 *jeongsugi*

watermelon / 수박 *subak*

weather / 날씨 *nalssi*

Wednesday / 수요일 *suyoil*

week / 주 *ju*

weekend / 주말 *jumal*

(to do something) well / 잘 *jal*

Western food / 양식 *yangsik*

wet / 젖다 *jeotda*

what / 무엇 *mueot*

when / 언제 *eonje*

where / 어디 *eodi*

which / 어느 *eoneu*

white / 하얀색 *hayansaek*

(to) withdraw money / 인출하다 *inchulhada*

who / 누구 *nugu*

whose / 누구의 *nuguui*

why / 왜 *wae*

wi-fi / 와이파이 *waipai*

window / 창문 *changmun*

wine / 와인 *wain*

winter / 겨울 *gyeoul*

witness / 목격자 *mokgyeokja*, 증인 *jeungin*

woman / 여자 *yeoja*

woman friend / 여자 사람 친구 (여사친) *yeoja saram chingu (yeosachin)*

women only / 여성전용 *yeoseong jeonyong*

won / 원 *won*

wound / 상처 *sangcheo*

wrist / 팔목 *palmok*

(to) write / 쓰다 *sseuda*

wrong / 틀리다 *teullida*

Y

year / 년 *nyeon*

yellow / 노란색 *noransaek*

yes / 예 *ye* , 네 *ne*

yesterday / 어제 *eoje*

younger man (younger brother) / 남동생 *namdongsaeng*

younger woman (younger sister) / 여동생 *yeodongsaeng*

Credits

Authors Irene Schokker, Lauren Kies, and Rachel van den Berg

Publisher Hyunggeun Kim
Editor Woo Jiwon
Copy Editor Anna Bloom
Designer Cynthia Fernández